Praise

"Set in southern Italy, *The Salty Mountain* is a captivating historical narrative of a family and their journey to America, weaving together the stories of three generations of women: Nonna, Mammuccèlla, and Angela. A series of visceral missives transports us back to an uncertain and bucolic world, and a people driven by the power of religious faith, witchcraft, and the miraculous force of life. Inside the mountainous landscape we encounter tales of lost church bells and the German occupation, meet a fortune-telling parrot and the postwoman who always carries a silver whistle. There is birth, death, survival, and prayer.

In creating *The Salty Mountain*, D'Arezzo and Appel have produced a lyrical work that is utterly captivating and deeply human."

— Susanna Crossman

Susanna Crossman is a British writer based in France. She is represented by Craig Literary. *More at:*
susanna-crossman.squarespace.com
@crossmansusanna

THE SALTY MOUNTAIN

THE SALTY MOUNTAIN

Angela D'Arezzo with Cathy Appel

Overtime Dance Foundation, Inc.
New York

ISBN 978-1-7335013-0-9

Book design by Christine Picone and Robert Wilson, Jr.;
design consultant Richard Figiel
Cover painting and illustrations by Naima Rauam

Printed in the United States
First Edition

For My Parents Rosa and Antonio D'Arezzo
whose love and devotion sustain me still
and Gallo Matese and Vairano Patenora
forever in my heart

—Angela D'Arezzo

For My Grandmother Catherine
whom I never met,
and My Mother
who missed her every day

—Cathy Appel

Table of Contents

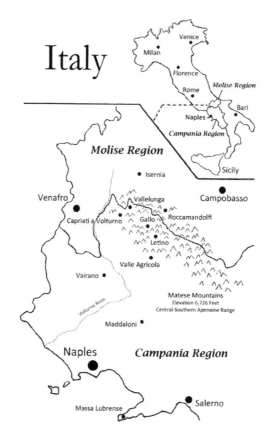

Italy

Venice

Milan

Florence

Rome

Molise Region

Bari

Naples

Campania Region

Sicily

Molise Region

• Isernia

Vallelunga

Venafro

Campobasso

Capriati a Volturno

Gallo

Roccamandolfi

Letino

Valle Agricola

Vairano

Volturno River

Matese Mountains
Elevation 6,726 Feet
Central-Southern Apennine Range

Maddaloni

Naples

Campania Region

Massa Lubrense

Salerno

Preface

Writing a book that came to be called *The Salty Mountain* was a long process. It began 20 years ago, in the late 1990s, when Angela D'Arezzo had the opportunity to pursue her long held desire to participate in the arts, especially dance and theater, through the National Theater Workshop of the Handicapped. At that time, Angela asked me to choreograph a dance for her so that she could contribute to an event with NTWH, and we worked together to create a piece that she performed in her motorized wheelchair at NTWH's black box theater on Elizabeth Street in Manhattan.

It was inspiring to see Angela's performance experiences grow beyond NTWH and the summer 1998 workshops she attended at the NTWH-Crosby campus in Belfast, Maine, where she had the chance to perform a Tango. Back in New York City, she continued performing for a couple of years with Kala (Krista) Smith in her Visible Theater venues. Through Smith's True Story Project, Angela worked with professionals on creating short monologues based on true stories for performance. She again approached me for assistance, hoping to expand her monologues. Their brevity frustrated her, and she was eager to do more performing.

Through regular conversations with her parents on the one hand, and then with me, at my computer, talking with her on the other, ideas for Angela's stories developed. We talked about her early years, often researching details in order to fill in memory gaps and to expand the material. I listened to Angela speak, asked her questions and encouraged her to concentrate on specific details that could lead to a cohesive narrative. After the True Story Project ended, we kept going and Angela talked about wanting a book.

It became necessary to provide a context for the narrative fragments by examining the history, not only of Angela's family, but also of her parents' villages in the Campania Region of Italy, Gallo Matese and Vairano

Patenora, and of Italy, itself. This involved teasing out details and themes, so that whole stories could emerge, be shaped and written down.

The process of excavating material was laborious. But, at the same time, delving into the subject matter ignited Angela's motivation to keep pursuing the stories further. Simultaneously, the work enlivened her connection to Gallo. For these reasons, I chose to stay with the project as its scope expanded far beyond the initial monologues. Our meetings continued, and I was able to shape what I was writing into sequential paragraphs. The depth of Angela's attachment to her family moved me and I was inspired by the history of the life she knew before coming to America.

The bravery of Angela and her parents became an underlying theme, as did the extent to which Angela had been able to make necessary and sometimes difficult transitions throughout her life, to accommodate the unexpected and to manage change and loss. As the years working on the project progressed, I accepted the increasing demands that my writing the book entailed. The responsibility challenged me to write with as much precision and accuracy as possible with regard both to Angela's feelings, as well as to the actual truths reflected in the information being gathered. For Angela, the desire to have a book that expressed and interpreted the devotion she felt to her childhood and family, especially her mother and father, strengthened as the manuscript grew. It was a welcome relief when structural ideas I was trying began to work and the title *The Salty Mountain* came to me.

While we chipped away at finding, developing and clarifying family stories, I encouraged Angela to utilize her interest in languages by checking words in her native dialect from Gallo for correct usage and spelling, as well as the ways in which her speech changed according to where she lived. We questioned whether we would use dialect, but Angela's commitment to the Gallese dialect and our realization that it was in danger of being lost fueled the effort to gather information, so that we would be able to make the best decision. Angela also worked hard to be sure any formal Italian used in the book was correct.

What began as a way for Angela to fulfill her yearning for dance and theater, by providing a vessel through which she could embody her love of performance, connection and beauty in an ongoing project, evolved into *The Salty Mountain*. A chronicle of events that are humorous and deeply poignant, the book is a choreography of culture, geography and personalities, past and present, that revolve around the importance of home and family.

Angela's commitment to this project remained un-daunted. I am grateful to her, as are many others, for her passion. *The Salty Mountain* is a tribute to Angela's family and place of birth. It was a privilege to retrieve and write these stories and to support Angela in embracing and sharing her remarkable history.

Catherine Appel
May 12, 2018

Introduction

BETWEEN THE GARDEN AND THE OLIVE TREES

My early years were spent traveling with my parents and our growing family between my mother's village of Gallo Matese and *il borgo*,[1] the old section of my father's town, Vairano Patenora. Connected by family and the natural world of the Campania Region in southern Italy, I thrived in body and spirit between time spent in the magical garden of my grandmother's house in the foothills of the Matese Mountains, and my paternal grandfather's home 31 kilometers south in the larger town of Vairano with its giant castle and majestic olive trees.

Years ago in Italy, if you were raised in a small village

---

1. A small hamlet.

and from a poor, uneducated family that made a living through farming, you were considered low-class. My introduction to this inequality happened when I was in third grade and felt shame when I was overlooked in class because of discrimination that existed between the poor and the wealthier people of the village. For years, I carried that shame and felt ambivalence about my childhood.

Now that I am older and understand the beauty of being born and raised in a rustic village like Gallo Matese, I see what a blessing it was to live in nature surrounded by the wonder of four seasons, where everything I ate was organic, and I saw the sun shine over the garden as I looked east out the small window above our bed in the sleeping loft that I shared with my sisters. Every morning at the crack of dawn, Zia Rosa's rooster would perch on top of the gate between her barn and our house and crow *chicchirichì, chicchirichì,* and I knew it was time to get up.

In the springtime, when the sparrows returned to the garden, there was a slight chirping early every morning that would grow to a melodious chorus throughout the day. The birds were busy making nests under the terra-cotta roof tiles and in between the branches of the sour plum trees. I enjoyed watching the newborns with their tiny beaks wide open, waiting to be fed, and the colorful wings of butterflies fluttering all over the garden as I tried to catch one. I was so excited when the cherry tree blossomed into a pink bouquet of flowers that eventually turned into cherries. Searching for pairs of cherries, I would remove them from the branches very carefully to make sure they didn't come apart, place the stems over my ears, and shake my head making believe I had on dangly red earrings. The bees deposited their honey on the trunk of the cherry tree, and I scraped the honeycomb from the crust to taste the sweet gold on my fingers.

I can still hear the sound of the plums falling onto the ground from the tall trees as I ran quickly to grab one and clean it with my hands, eager for a juicy taste. Ahh, the smell of earth when it rained and the surprise of rainbows that sometimes appeared, arching from our garden into Zia 'Ngelélla's[2] garden. Taken with the red, orange, yellow, green, and violet glow, I stood watching long after it had disappeared hoping the rainbow would return.

After school, I would run across the street to a nearby field and throw myself down in the tall green grass among the red poppies with my arms and legs akimbo. Lying there, I looked up at the blue sky, alert for the rare sight

2. Dialect for the name Angela.

of an airplane or listened intently for the hum of the occasional car. How often did I sit in that crisp grass picking the petals from daisies: "He loves me, he loves me not"? Dry hot days, Mamma in the fields with her knife, digging up the chicory and chamomile that grew wild. Later, their flowers drying on the dividing wall of the garden to make a soothing tea that was given to newborns with colic or to children and adults for stomach cramps.

Not far from the school was a tunnel where my friends and I often went without permission. Purple violets and moss grew inside, and spring water surged from the ground. I would bend down to make a hole with my hand so I could suck the cold water through without getting mud all over my face. At one end of the tunnel, which was at a crossroad called *ru Spressòdie*, or the shortcut, there was a big scarecrow in the middle of a field to prevent sparrows from eating the crops.

Surrounded by animals—chickens, roosters, horses, pigs, cows, sheep, insects, birds—our lives were imbued with superstition as inexplicable things happened. We all knew about *il malocchio*, the evil eye, and that *Zozómbola*, the town wicked witch was there to put a spell on anyone she didn't like, and especially on their newborn children.

Looking back now, it seems to me that life in my

Italian village was joyful, simple but satisfying, where neighbors all knew one another and fruit was freshly picked from trees, vegetables from the garden, and milk squeezed that same day from the cow. As the oldest child, I don't share the same past as my siblings. I lived in Italy until I was ten, and I'm so grateful for those years. The child I was yesterday still lives in the adult I am today, and nothing can take away those moments. That time in my life has become even more precious to me now, because after so many years in the United States, I finally returned to visit Gallo Matese. No longer a poor village, the new generation has built modern houses with indoor stoves and bathrooms. Women no longer balance pots of water on their heads while carrying buckets full in each hand, and laundry is not washed in the village fountain. But despite the suburban atmosphere, the beauty of the village surrounded by mountains remains otherworldly.

I always said to myself, "I wish to visit my hometown and see where I was born one more time before I die." Now that I've done that, I want to go back again and again. I want to tell the unforgettable stories of how people struggled to make a living by farming, and how men left their families behind to go to Germany, Switzerland, Argentina, Venezuela, and the United States, where work was plentiful so they could send money back to help their families survive. Eventually, even though my Papà didn't want to leave, my own family moved abroad. Our journey only happened because of the firmness of Mamma's decision that if Papà wouldn't come, she would leave Gallo alone with her four children to join the rest of her family in New York City.

The Salty Mountain tells some of the stories that were passed from my grandmother to my mother and then to me.

Note to Reader

There are many dialects spoken throughout Italy that make speech very different from formal Italian. For instance, in the Gallese dialect, the letter *e* is pronounced only if it has an accent. There are also variations between formal Italian words such as *zia* for *aunt* and *zio* for *uncle* in Italian, which in dialect become *zi* for either aunt or uncle.

Gallo's dialect is a polyglot mix of Italian and Bulgarian. However, my speech was even more mixed, because we traveled back and forth between Gallo and my father's town, Vairano, which has its own dialect. The first three years of my life were spent in Gallo, and I called my mother *Mà*. In Vairano, from age four to six, I called her *Mammà*. Back in Gallo from age seven to ten, she was *Mòma* and *Mò* for short.

It was the same with my father. In Gallo he was *Tata*, and in Vairano, *Papà*. When we returned to Gallo, my mother didn't want us to use *Tata*, so she modified *Papà* to *Papò*. When we came to the United States, I changed *Mammà* to *Mammuccèlla* (I think I devised this term of affection out of my need to acknowledge all that she endured before leaving Italy), sometimes *Mòma, Mò, Mammuccè, Mommy,* and *Mà*. My father is still *Papò*, but I also call him *Papucciéglie*, or *Papucciê* for short.

The reader will find another inconsistency here with my mother's speech, because her dialect was not spoken in the convent. The years she spent there altered her speech so that, for seemingly random words, she uses Italian. Perhaps because it was my first language, the Gallese dialect has stayed strong in my mind and is something I hold dear to my heart above my other languages of traditional Italian, English, and Spanish.

Chapter I

AMERICA

It is September 1970. We are in an Alitalia airplane on our way to America. I love the plane ride. It is my first time. I've never even seen one up close. We are the first members of my family to fly to America. Everyone else made a three-week voyage by ship. All the passengers on the plane are Italian, so no English is being spoken. Each of us is looking forward to the same dream of prosperity as we watch movies, sleep, and eat. We're going to America! After eight hours in the air, we finally land at Kennedy International Airport at seven p.m. But my family's journey actually began years before.

The only way I knew my maternal grandmother, Maria Castaldo, was through the packages she sent from the United States and my mother's stories. In those days, Gallo Matese had only one post woman. Her nickname was Signora de Lione, and she walked through the town delivering mail with a silver whistle on a cord around her neck, and she would blow the whistle to announce that she had a delivery. Hearing the whistle, Mamma would run out of the house and meet Signora de Lione at our front gate. All the villagers did this.

When my grandparents were in their early fifties, they left their roots behind and moved to America with my aunts and uncle. My grandfather's brother, Benefàzie,[3] was already in the United States and had offered to sponsor the entire family, but because my mother was married, she was ineligible, so we were left back in Gallo Matese in my grandmother's house. Finally, we settled into one place, but it felt as if the rest of the family had abandoned us.

The first time my mamma got the message that there was a package waiting in the post office to be picked up, I was only one year old and had no idea what this meant. When Papà was not working, it was his responsibility to walk up the steep hill to get the delivery and then carry the heavy package on his shoulder back down to our home.

3. Dialect for the name Bonifacio.

Aside from being the place where we picked up packages, the post office served the function of a bank, because at that time Gallo did not have one. Most people were poor and uneducated, but those with money kept it in the post office, where few of the personnel were from Gallo and the rest commuted by car from other towns. This was in an area called *ru Còlle* near *l'asilo*, the nursery school, run by nuns, that my sisters and I attended.

Mamma would be so excited when Papà came in the door with the package that she'd start opening it right away. At first, I didn't pay much attention, but by the time I was two, when a package arrived, I joined right in saying, "Give me, give me," as I started helping. Every six months, my grandmother sent a package, and every seven days she sent a letter with five dollars enclosed. By the time I was three years old, I knew who Signora de Lione was, and whenever I saw her on our pathway blowing her whistle, I jumped up and down and chanted, "Nonna's package is coming, Nonna's package is coming!" and "Mammà, Mammà, answer me! Nonna's package is coming!" Most of the time, it was only a letter, but this didn't stop me. Once, I was napping, and when I woke up my mother told me, "Angelina, the package from America has arrived," and I started right in with my melody: "It's

3

here, it's here!" I ran and stood by the package, waiting anxiously for Mamma to open it, since Nonna had sewn it in burlap, using heavy white thread all around so that only a knife could break the stitches one by one.

I was bursting inside for it to finally open so I could dig into the package with small quick hands. I took out clothes so fast and threw them on the floor. When I saw something I liked, I wanted to try it on immediately and demanded, "Mammà, Mammà, stop! Try this dress on me!" She would stop and help me try on the dress. Satisfied, I'd give it back to her so she could put it away in the storage box with the rest of my siblings' clothes, since we didn't have a dresser.

Nonna never sent a package without candy and other goodies like Wrigley's Spearmint gum, M&Ms, heart-shaped chocolates, sour candies, sugar, coffee, Stella D'Oro cookies, honey, Ronzoni spaghetti, Johnson & Johnson baby powder, little girls' hats with flowers on top for spring and white furry pom-pom hats that tied under the chin for winter. There were beaded chains in different colors and socks, underwear, blankets, skirts, and shirts. I got particularly excited when I saw the beaded necklaces, and I'd put them all around my neck at once and trot off next door to Zia Rosa's shouting, "Look! Look!" She always

4

made a fuss, telling me how beautiful they were. This delighted me, and then I would happily go back home, take them off, and store them in a small wooden box that I'd found around the house and kept for my jewels. Whenever I went into town with Mamma, I wore my beads, and the villagers who saw me would admire them and say, "I can tell that you have a grandmother in America." Rumor had it that, even as a small child, I was very organized, and God forbid if anyone touched my things! I also loved candies and would be so overwhelmed, I wouldn't know which one to try first. I would unwrap them and try one candy at a time, and, if I liked it, I ate it. If I didn't like it, I spit it out.

As time went on, I learned from my mother that my grandparents had to be permanent residents in the United States for nine and a half years to be able to file for citizenship. We had no choice but to wait and see what the future would bring.

Chapter 2

ROOTS

In 1928, when Nonna was twenty-one, my nonno, Giovanni Cioffi, fell in love with her. They lived in the same village, and were married after a brief courtship. Nonna's mother owned fifty sheep and gave five to the young couple as a wedding gift. Years later, when my mammuccèlla was a girl, it was her responsibility after school to take the sheep to graze on top of L'Acchia della Macchia, a mountain not far from the house, where my grandparents owned a small plot of land. There, she did her homework leaning against a rock. It was a wonderful place to recite aloud: "one times two equals two; two times two equals four"; and so on.

One sheep was more special than the rest, adorable and obedient, so my mamma named her Bianca, after her favorite nun from nursery school. Walking along the path up the mountain with the sheep, she would take out her rosary beads and pray. When she reached the top and settled down to work, she whispered in Bianca's ear, "*La bella ciavarrèlla*, my beautiful lamb, don't gò too far. I have to do my homework and when I call, come back to me." She always carried a little piece of bread in her pocket and would stop every now and then to tear off a scrap and call, "Bianca, I have bread for you," but all the other sheep followed. Mamma knew how to talk to the sheep, but the bread helped and so did Bianca because she was like a person. Singing was another of Mamma's pastimes up on the mountain, where she serenaded the sheep with her favorite hymns.

The Catholic religion was the common source of faith in Gallo Matese in those days, and everyone went to church on Sundays and observed all the religious holidays, like Saints' days, Christmas, the Epiphany, and Easter. Each Italian village had a patron saint that protected the town; Gallo's was Saint Anthony.[4] Every year on June 13th, there

4.   In the United States, St. Anthony is popularly known as the patron of lost things. In Gallo Matese, we prayed to him for many reasons, especially fertility, and for young women to find husbands.

was a mass in his honor followed by a celebration with a band and a procession leading to the town square. Ahead of time, the priest would arrange a crew with several men to lift the statue of Saint Anthony down from its dome and mount it on a portable wooden platform covered with a white cloth. Then four men at a time carried the saint on their shoulders out of the church and through the cobblestone streets of town.

The procession began with nuns leading a double line of seven- and eight-year-old children, all wearing their First Communion outfits and singing religious songs. Parishioners who were members of the Catholic Club held religious images and prayed aloud. Then came the priest, the mayor, wearing a banner of the Italian flag across his chest, and the musicians. Sounds of cymbals, trombones, and clarinets filled the air, along with firecrackers paving the way for St. Anthony and other saints, like St. Bonifacio, Our Lady of Grace, and Madonna of the Rosary. The rest of the worshippers joined at the end, some, like Zia Rosa, carrying a baby or toddler dressed in brown tunics like St. Anthony's, and interspersed were other believers, barefoot, in desperate need, sobbing loudly and lamenting, asking for grace.

Even though I was small and it was many years ago,

I remember the excitement of wearing new clothes and walking in those processions while the older villagers looked down from their balconies lined with terra-cotta pots brimming with red geraniums, and, as the statue of St. Anthony passed, everyone made the sign of the cross. Tired but excited, we would return to the church, where the priest blessed the Sacrament and thanked everyone involved: the *carabinieri*,[5] the crew, and the entire village.

One of the most faithful, my nonna never missed a procession and would stand beside the road praying with her rosary to St. Anthony as the worshippers passed by. If it had not been for her arthritis, she would have been among them. Nonna did not just pray when she was in desperate need, but said the rosary every day.

5.   Policemen.

Chapter 3

MAMMUCCÈLLA'S BIRTH

My mother was born April 30, 1937, the third of six children. Her parents were Maria Castaldo and Giovanni Cioffi, and Deméneca was their eldest. Then came Resàrie, dialect for Rosario, who was three when my nonna became pregnant with my mother. He got seriously ill and remained critical until after she was born. Afraid her son wasn't going to live, Nonna waited to baptize her newborn. This meant my mother had no name for the first forty-four days of her life, because in those days, babies were given their names at their christening. Sadly, Resàrie did not survive, and so my mother was named Rosa, after him.

Like all of her generation in Gallo, Nonna believed heavily in *le ianòre*, or witchcraft, and, according to her, a town witch took the baby's life. One night, out of nowhere, a black cat appeared in Nonna's house, and she could not shoo him away. Trying to get the cat to leave, she hit it with a broomstick, only realizing she'd hurt his right front leg when she saw him limp on his way out the door. The next morning, Nonna went to the field to cut grass for the animals to eat, and on her way home, she met a *paisana*[6] whose right arm was bandaged. Nonna asked, "Hey, what happened, you broke your arm?"

The woman replied, "You broke it last night, and if you want your children to be safe, watch them carefully at night."

Nonna panicked because, at the time, Resàrie had been ill for four months. She ran home to find that his fever had risen dangerously high. Nonna thought about what the woman had said and believed that either out of envy or spite, *despiétte*, dialect for *dispetto*, she'd performed witchcraft on Resàrie.

Nonna sent her husband, Giovanni, to Longano, which is ten miles from Gallo, where there was a master sorcerer, *Il Magone delle Streghe*—the magician of the witches—to have him reverse the spell. It took a while to

6. Neighbor from the same town.

walk to Longano, and when Giovanni reached Il Magone's house, he was told, "You came too late. Your son is already dead." When Giovanni arrived home, he found the baby dressed in white and laid out on the kitchen table, which was set up like a bed covered with a white sheet. On it was a white towel folded in the middle where Resàrie lay overnight with Nonna sitting by his side.

In those days, the tradition in Gallo was that the baptismal godmother was considered a second mother, and, by obligation, was responsible for buying the baby's coffin and carrying him to the church and cemetery. Resàrie died on June 13th, the Feast of St. Anthony, and on the next day, after the final prayer and blessing from the priest, his godmother put him in the coffin, placed it on her head, and left for the church with the mourners following. After the funeral service, the small coffin was again placed on the godmother's head, and the procession walked to the cemetery.

This tragedy meant that my mother's birth was not celebrated. In fact, Nonna was so preoccupied and depressed from the time *la piccola*[7] *Rosa* was born, that she couldn't care for the infant. After Resàrie's death, it got

7. Little.

worse. Nonna wrapped Rosa in *ru fasciatùre*, a kind of cloth diaper, and placed her in a cradle on the floor next to her bed. The bed was so high that she couldn't see the cradle.

After several days, a neighbor became suspicious and asked my nonna, "How come I don't see you washing any of the baby's clothes?" When she didn't get an answer, she went to the town hall to report the situation to the authorities, and the mayor went to check.

"Maria," said the mayor, "what are you doing with your baby?" He saw that the infant was neglected, and immediately sent for the town midwife, who was unable to remove the diaper from the baby. It was stuck, and Rosa's skin came off with the cloth.

Those who saw her at the time said she looked like *ne cuniglie*, a rabbit, because she was so malnourished. They soaked Rosa in tepid water to remove the rotting cloth, and she developed a contagious cough called *pertosse*, or whooping cough. The midwife gave her cough medicine with a dropper, and suggested that Rosa be fed chamomile tea in place of milk, since Nonna wasn't lactating.

At this time, the mayor asked Nonna, "Do you want to keep this baby or should we put her in the orphanage?" This brought Nonna to her senses.

Chapter 4

NONNA'S MIRACLES

Fortunately, Nonna's faith was strong. She and her young family lived at the piazza right by the main church, Ave Gratia Plena, built in 1642. She loved to be so near the church bells, especially forty days after Easter, when The Pilgrimage of La Madonna dei Lattani was observed. Her heart pounded with excitement when everyone met by the church at four a.m., and at four thirty, the ringing of the bells, *dill-dall, dill-dall, dill-dall,* signified the worshippers' departure on their long pilgrimage to the sanctuary in Roccamonfina.

After Resàrie's death, when Rosa was a fragile newborn, the priest, Don Michele, asked my grandfather, Giovanni, to carry the cross for The Pilgrimage of La Madonna dei

Lattani, a miraculous saint in the church of Roccamonfina, a town of a thousand inhabitants located thirty-two miles east of Gallo. The church was isolated on top of a slope two miles up the dormant volcanic mountain, Lactanorum, set like a diamond in nature's greenery and surrounded by a grove of chestnut trees that bloomed every spring.

Carrying the cross was an honor Giovanni accepted, and he set off early in the morning, leaving his wife and newborn daughter home in bed. He carried a handmade medium-sized cross used just for that devotion, made from green wood and wrapped with a white handkerchief tied with a pink bow around each of its points. Another villager was assigned to hold *la campanella*, or small bell, he would ring from time to time, especially as they approached a new town, to alert the villagers of their arrival so they could join in. This part of the pilgrimage was twelve hours long, and after five hours, everyone took a break in the town of Marzano Appio. In Marzano there was a special outdoor rest area where the pilgrims could sit on the ground or on the steps leading to the fourteenth-century church dell'Annunziata and eat whatever they had brought for lunch. After resting, they continued until a cacophony of church bells welcomed them to the sanctuary of the miraculous Madonna dei Lattani in Roccamonfina.

The story goes that, right after the litany began, Nonna felt a sudden wetness all over her chest. When she looked at herself, she wasn't wet, but her breasts were filled with milk and she immediately started to breastfeed her infant. Nonna believed it was a miracle. She promptly made a promise to La Madonna to join the twelve-hour pilgrimage the following year, and this is how, at one year of age, my mamma was transported in a wooden cradle tied to the saddle of a horse that her mother led all the way to Roccamonfina. Of course, being a beautiful baby, all the young women on the pilgrimage fought to carry her until they reached the sanctuary. Then Nonna took off her shoes with la piccola Rosa in her arms and walked barefoot into the church, praising La Madonna dei Lattani, the Regina Mundi and patron of breast milk for all pregnant women.

For years after this, breast milk was an important theme in my family. I was born in March of 1960, and even then, there was no other way in our village to nourish a newborn. Three months before my birth, another baby named Angela was born, but her mother got seriously sick and was hospitalized with pneumonia for six months until she died. During this time her Zia Francesca, who was single, dedicated herself totally to the baby and engaged townspeople to help. After I was born, my mother, who had plenty of milk, nursed us both. I believe God works in mysterious ways, so that Nonna's prayer to La Madonna dei Lattani resulted in both her and Rosa having an abundance of breast milk.

Another of Nonna's miracles happened when her next-to-last child and only living son, Demìnecu, dialect for Domenico, got very sick as a baby with a disease called *la malattia di San Donato*, a kind of epilepsy. Until the 1960s, in Gallo, when a baby was born, its whole body was wrapped around and around, from the neck down, with a thick white cotton cloth like a bandage—or, better yet, like a mummy. It was believed that this would make newborns' bodies straight. One day, when my Zio Demìnecu was eight months old, Nonna unwrapped him for bathing as part of the daily routine and noticed that his arms and legs were twisting. Neighbors advised my grandmother to follow a remedy they believed was a cure, and they helped her immerse him in tepid water with *male* door keys placed in his hands. In those days, two types of keys existed, male and female, the male without a hole, the female with. Keys were used according to whether the door had a male or female lock. Male keys were also a symbol of devotion, but they did not help Zi Demìnecu.

22

A few months later, after trying all the remedies, Nonna put her faith in a saint called San Donato. He was a bishop and a martyr well known for healing children with deformities, and his statue is in the church of San Sebastiano in La Rocca,[8] a town that was nearly a six-hour walk from Gallo if you took the paths between the mountains. Nonna took Demìnecu there, and the monks, *i monaci*, led them inside the chapel to the statue of San Donato, where, hung from the ceiling by three giant chains, was a large Roman scale. The monks lifted Demìnecu into the scale and weighed him. They then instructed his parents to go back to their hometown and take up a collection for an amount of food determined by the number of kilos he weighed. A week later, they were to return with the baby and whatever food was collected.

Nonna brought back more than was required. Neighbors gave her whatever they could—grain, beans, potatoes, and eggs. The food filled two burlap sacks that were tied on either side of the horse, and then the wooden cradle with Demìnecu inside was tied to the saddle. Rosa, who was only three at the time, was tied to the rump of the

8. The official name of this town is Roccamandolfi, but in Nonna's day, the locals simply called it La Rocca.

horse so she would not fall, while my grandparents, both on foot, led the horse. When they arrived, they unloaded and brought the goods inside the chapel. The monks directed my nonna to untie the child, and they placed him on the scale to be weighed again. When the monks took Demìnecu off the scale, Nonna reached to grab the child for fear he would fall, but a monk said, "Signora, put him down and let him walk." Nonna, hesitant, put her baby down while balancing him with her hands to prevent him from falling. Instead, he started walking and running all around the chapel, with his arms and legs moving freely like any other child. Another miracle had happened.

A tough woman, Nonna hardly ever smiled. She kept her guard up, letting nothing slide by, and never backed down from a fight if it involved her principles. For instance, the time her neighbor, Zia Rosa, who many years later became my mamma's best friend, had a leak in her roof tiles that dripped onto Nonna's cherry tree. She asked her to fix the leak, but Zia Rosa ignored her, so Nonna went right to *il comune*, the town council, to enlist the help of the carabinieri, and the problem was quickly resolved. Not one to worry what people thought of her, Nonna never hesitated to take action.

Chapter 5

EARLY HISTORY
OF VAIRANO

The town of Vairano Patenora is located in the Campania Region of southern Italy, in the province of Caserta. It is historical not just because it is my papà's place of birth and one hour away from my mamma's town, Gallo Matese, but because of its medieval origins and a castle built with mortar and stone on top of a large hill dating from the 900s. No one knows the exact beginning of Vairano Patenora. However, there is archeological evidence, such as tombstones, bricks, and abandoned ruins that lead historians to believe the Romans founded Vairano.

Vairano Patenora is large, not rural like Gallo Matese, but I know both towns well because, as a child, we were just like *i zingari*, or the Romani. At least, this is how I describe my early childhood.

When my parents first married, they lived in il borgo the old section of Vairano, with my paternal grandfather and uncle, but it became too crowded, so they moved back to Gallo. From then on, they traveled back and forth between the two towns, depending on where there was enough room for the growing family and whether my papà had the opportunity to work. This is how I came to live as a traveler until I was seven years old and we finally settled in Gallo Matese, in my grandmother's house after she moved to the United States and the renovation of the house was finished.

Historically, Italy did not exist as a political entity in the Late Middle Ages/early modern period, from around 300 to 700 AD, and continuing well beyond 1000 AD. Before its unification, Italy was divided into smaller cities, states, territories, and new nations owned by different countries. The Roman Empire began in the eighth century BC, but there is no definitive date for its end. In 395 AD, the Roman Empire was divided into East and West, and the Western Empire lasted until 476 AD, and the Byzantium,[9] or East, survived until 1453 AD.

9.   An ancient Greek city.

After the sack of Rome in 410 AD, and during the barbaric invasions, nobles began to build fortifications and castles throughout the area, including Vairano, to better defend themselves.

Vairano existed before recorded history. Evidence of ancient dwellings downhill indicates that people lived there before the castle was built. With the barbaric invasions, inhabitants began to relocate uphill to find shelter, and eventually the castle was built and most people lived within its grounds. During the feudal era, Vairano was sold many times. It wasn't until the 1200s when the Normanni[10] took over, establishing their rule, that the town acquired stability and il borgo was expanded. The castle was then modified to give it a Normanni style. For self-defense, a wall containing sixteen towers was built around the castle. In the 1300s, the Aragonesi[11] bought Vairano, and the castle was again modified, this time with Aragonesi characteristics, and San Tommaso's, our church, was built.

During the Middle Ages, the population had to pay a tax called *la tassa del camino*, meaning that for every house with a chimney, you paid a tax. In order to afford this,

10. Normans.
11. Spanish.

two or three families comprised of siblings and in-laws often lived in one household. Another aspect of peasant life during the Middle Ages is reflected in a legend about weddings. Marriages were traditionally celebrated with religious rituals between people of the same social rank, but the duke is said to have intervened and put into effect the law *Jus Primae Noctis*, which obligated all brides to spend their wedding night with him. Consequently, the duke's soldiers guarded wedding banquets, and if, at times, a bride succeeded in running away and was caught, she was severely punished or put to death. Despite these hardships, Vairano slowly grew from 150 to 300 families. Marchese Bartolomeo Geremia was the first mayor of Vairano in 1806, when the town council and municipality were formed. It was at this time that official recordkeeping began tracking births as follows: "Identity card #86 of Geremia Pasquale of Bartolomeo and Annina Ferraro, born October 1, 1817 at Vairano Patenora near a ditch where his mother worked."

Feudalism started to end in Naples in 1759 with the arrival of Ferdinand IV, the first Bourbon king of Naples and Sicily. He created *il Regno delle Due Sicilie*, the Reign of the Two Sicilies, out of many smaller kingdoms, uniting the area from Sicily to the Campania Region. In 1860,

Vittorio Emanuele II, the king of Savoia in the northwest part of Italy, asked Garibaldi (called the Hero of the Two Worlds), to command the revolutionary rebellion. As a result, Garibaldi led approximately a thousand volunteers in red shirts, called the Expedition of the Thousand, to conquer the Kingdom of the Two Sicilies. This campaign ended with Garibaldi's triumphant arrival in Naples, the final surrender of the last Bourbon king, Francis II, and the annexation of the Two Sicilies to the new Kingdom of Italy. The Vairanesi will tell you that the unification of Italy happened in Vairano, exactly at Vairano Scalo, a subdivision of Vairano Patenora, near la Taverna Catena, on October 26, 1860, with the meeting between King Vittorio Emanuele II and Giuseppe Garibaldi.

Fortunately, the territory of Vairano has always been fertile, rich in agriculture, fields, farmland, and woods. During feudalism, when only the wealthy owned land, the peasants worked the nobles' farms for survival in exchange for food and shelter. Life was even more difficult for la plebe, plebes or serfs, living within the medieval hamlet, where the castle wall is so vast that there are three separate entrances in its circumference, each one a wide stone archway: Porta Oliva opens west to the setting sun; Porta di Mezzo is in the middle and faces southeast; and

33

Porta Castello, to the northeast, is nearest the castle itself. The fields and farms were all located outside il borgo, from one to six miles downhill from the castle, to where the land was flat. This meant the farmers who lived in the *tenute*[12] trudged downhill before dawn to work their noble's farms until sunset and then climbed back up every evening.

One of the dukes who owned the castle during this period directed his laborers downhill to remove and flatten superfluous rocks and create an open space that many years later was enlarged and planted with olive trees not far from the church now called Madonna di Loreto. Immediately outside the castle walls to the northeast, Pièsco[13] is a fertile area where sheep have grazed from 1200 AD until the present day, when there is now only one shepherd, nicknamed Maste Filippo. As the town grew, when people asked each other where they lived, those who stayed behind in the area by the castle would answer, "*'Ngòppa alla terra*," which is dialect for *above the earth*, while those who moved downhill, where they built houses and farmed their own land, lived in the shadow of the castle.

12.   Houses for the serfs who worked for the nobles.
13.   Dialect for *Pesco*.

Chapter 6

THE BELLS OF VAIRANO

The construction of the church named Madonna di Loreto, a black Madonna representing Mother Earth and often considered miraculous, began in 1632.[14] It was downhill from the castle in an open area like a piazza called Maronna 'iu Rito, or Mannurito, depending on which generation you are from. The closest route to get there from il borgo was through the middle door, Porta di Mezzo. This church's bell was called "the bell of the lost" because

14. The church existed until it was abandoned in the 1930s before WWII. It was not rebuilt until 2005, when Giovanni Malinconico, a man of means from a nearby area, prayed to La Madonna di Loreto to heal his beloved brother from cancer. He made a vow to rebuild the church if his brother's life was spared.

those who lost their way hunting game or collecting mushrooms, as well as in the northeast, where most of the farms were located, could hear the gongs throughout the southeast in the wooded mountainside. The sacristan, Pasquale Riccitiello, known to everyone as Zi Pascale Gliandenaro, nicknamed after the sound of the bell, rang it each noon to announce lunch.

Hearing the bell, all would stop work and gather to sit on the grass in the shade of a tree and untie the four points of *la sparra*, dialect for a four-pointed white cloth larger than a napkin and smaller than a tablecloth used to carry food.[15] The delicious aroma of lunches then filled the air—roasted peppers, beans, cheese, olives, homemade bread—and was shared freely among the peasants, creating a varied meal. After making the sign of the cross and muttering a prayer of gratitude, they would eat. Gliandenaro rang the bell again at five p.m. signaling the end of the workday. He lived in small quarters behind the church with his family. At harvest time, Gliandenaro visited each farm with a knapsack, and the farmers gave him a part of their

15. *La sparra* was carried by hand or tied onto the pole of a spade (*vanga*) or a hoe (*zappa*), or on a stick that rested over the shoulder. Women often twisted the *sparra* into a biscuit shape and placed it on their heads to carry *la cunchelina* (pot) filled with water.

produce, chickpeas, maize, flour, and potatoes, as payment for his labor.

A modest worker, Gliandenaro also rang the three bells of San Tommaso's Church,[16] located inside the walls of il borgo. At seven a.m. every morning, the soft sounds of the middle bell, called a *giorno*, indicated the start of the day's activities. It rang again at four p.m., a bit faster and for a longer period—thirty-three times—letting everyone know the end of the day was near.

Gliandenaro had to go back and forth between the two churches, keeping track of the different tones. He was illiterate, but had learned how to count from his mother. For his job, he developed a strategy of counting thirty-three grains of maize and, with every ring, would move a grain in order to maintain his accuracy. His thinking was not that precise, and, as he got older, age combined with the few glasses of wine he drank during the day made him forget the counts when he rang the bells. One day, ringing the bells at San Tommaso's, he didn't realize that he had rung only thirty, and several people in the town complained. After this, Gliandenaro was upset and went to

16.   A mass was said in San Tommaso's every Sunday until the 1960s, when the church was converted into a theater.

check his grain. He realized three pieces were missing, so he replaced them, but the mistake happened several more times until he finally realized the pigeons were eating the grain. After that, he used pebbles.

When the weather was bad with heavy rain, strong wind, thunder and lightning, Gliandenaro rang the bell to beseech the gale to make the storm stop. Even today, Italians make the sign of the cross and pray to Santa Barbara, guardian during thunderstorms, when the weather is bad. Many say, "Santa Barbara protects my family."

Vairano had many chapels devoted to various saints, but its main church was San Bartolomeo, named after the town's patron saint, who was chosen because he was considered to be miraculous. As one of the twelve apostles, called Il Padre dell'India, he went to the East starting in Arabia, and traveled all the way to Armenia, where he became a martyr when he was tortured and killed. To the Vairanesi, he was miraculous: they believed it was because of his apparition to the Saraceni, or Arabs, that their town was spared during the invasions. Construction on the church of San Bartolomeo began in 1779 and was completed in 1823, and the church still stands midway between il borgo (old Vairano) and the new Vairano, at the intersection of via San Nicola and via Raffaele Cirelli, uniting the old population with the new. The church is nearly 150 meters above sea level and faces west.

The Vairanesi's pride and strong faith in their patron saint generated an initiative to make the largest bell larger to give it a richer tone by adding gold. Contributions of gold such as wedding bands, bracelets, and baptism/confirmation chains were collected in 1860 and brought to the monastery of San Agostino.[17] Once the gold was gathered, it was fused with existing bronze to make the bell larger.

Celeste Verde, called Zi Celeste, was the sacristan who rang the bells of San Bartolomeo's church until he passed away in the 1960s. Volunteers took over until the church was modernized and the bells were set up to ring automatically.

After being fused, the largest of the three bells weighs more than 7.5 *quintali*, which is equivalent to 750 kg. Its tone is deep and heavy. The two smaller bells, one small and one medium, are located on either side. They all have different tones that blend together: the large bell has a tenor sound, *'ndon, 'ndon,* the second a medium tone, *'nden, 'nden, 'nden,* and the third a high tone *'ndin, 'ndin.*

17. It is now a high school.

41

On Sundays, holidays, and weddings, the bells ring at three fifteen-minute intervals, for five minutes at a time, to announce mass. Until the 1990s, three boys rang the church bells. One would ring the central and largest, pulling a cord by hand downstairs, while the other two boys climbed up to ring the smaller bells by their clappers, all three creating exciting sounds with rhythm and unifying tones, as if they were part of one musical instrument: *'ndon, 'ndon, 'ndin, 'ndin, 'nden, 'nden, 'ndon, 'ndin, 'nden, 'ndon.*

In 1911, a disaster occurred in San Bartolomeo's when the ceiling collapsed. Fortunately, Pasquale Cirelli, the son of Raffaele Cirelli,[18] and a famous architect, volunteered his work free of charge and used wooden rafters and cement, unknown in Vairano at the time, to repair the damage. His restoration work still holds today, but he is best known for building one of the bridges over the Po River, the longest river in Italy, which flows eastward across northern Italy from Monviso (in the Cottian Alps) to the Adriatic Sea near Venice and, in Vairano, for the construction of many roads and the installation of a large fountain with four spouts to collect spring water.

Since there are several churches in Vairano, years ago, if

18. Mayor of Vairano, 1854–1858.

you had a special function such as a wedding or a baptism, you were to use the church in your area. It was prohibited to use other churches. But the laws have changed, and the most popular church for weddings is Madonna di Loreto because it has lots of space for parking and a beautiful medieval view. Today, brides from nearby towns and cities make reservations well in advance to get married at Madonna di Loreto.

Chapter 7

PAPÀ'S CHILDHOOD

Papà, Antonio D'Arezzo, was born and raised in Vairano but also had a strong connection to Rocca Vecchia because it is where his mother, Angela (I am her namesake), had lived before marrying his father, my grandfather Bartolomeo. Rocca Vecchia is a gigantic wooded area of large oak trees about four miles from the towns of Vairano and Pratella. Residents lived in *masserie*, rustic farmhouses that were distanced from each other and hidden from view by the forest surrounding them, which was filled with wild animals such as boar, badgers, and predatory birds. Throughout his childhood, Papà's mother regularly brought him there to visit her family.

When my father was a boy, the only way to get to

Rocca Vecchia was to cross the deep rough waters of the long Fiume (river) Volturno on horseback. For this reason and its muddy trails that were dangerous to travel on, especially in bad weather, Rocca Vecchia was an inadequate place to live.

The story of Rocca Vecchia's origin attributes it to a man nicknamed Il Colonello, who was a retired colonel from the military. He came from another town and bought property in the woods, where he built ten houses in which people lived rent-free on the second floor. In return, every household had to cultivate his land and take care of the animals that lived in stables on the ground floor. Papà's cousin Guglielmina and her parents were one of the original families on Il Colonello's land. It was a rugged life, because the dangerous river sometimes flooded and there were no stores, which made travel to nearby towns a necessity despite the risks.

Each family living on Il Colonello's property was assigned animals to raise and land to farm. They were responsible for taking the animals to the fields, cultivating the land, raising both crops and newborn livestock, and selling them at *la fièra*, the local outdoor flea market. Proceeds were divided among the peasants and the colonel, with each receiving a percentage. The only animals not sold were the chickens and sometimes rabbits. Papà said, "If the colonel received one live chicken per year, it was a lot." The rest were killed to make dishes such as savory chicken soup. The same was true of the rabbits. The peasants also used the vegetables for their meals, so there was little produce left over to be sold. As he talked about the farm, still vivid in his eyes, Papà recalled the pungent aroma of big, hot, red, juicy tomatoes. Mammuccèlla added, "Living in the masseria is like being the super of a building in New York City; you live rent-free and get paid for the job."

Papà didn't like Rocca Vecchia, saying, "Everyone who lived there either survived or they died." Guglielmina was Papà's favorite cousin (on his mother's side). She was ten years older, and even though they lived far apart, she remained attached to him. Part of her inexplicable deep affection for my Papà led her to be the only relative from that area who risked traveling all the way to 'Ngòppa alla Terra to visit him. Guglielmina also always begged Papà to come and stay at the masseria for four or five days. One day, during a visit to Vairano, she kept trying to convince him to go home with her. Part of him wanted to go, and part of him didn't. It was already after six p.m. in the wintertime, and there were no streetlights. At only seven years old, he was afraid of the dark, but she grabbed him and put him in the horse and buggy. The driver who had brought her was one of her neighbors and he was drunk. The river that had to be crossed was dangerous, and Papà never forgot how Guglielmina told him over and over, "'Ndniù" (dialect for Antonio), "don't be afraid." Papà said, "No!" She said, "Yes!" and finally, she grabbed him. All my little Papà could think about was the dark, and as he tells it, "I fought for my life!"

On the way to Rocca Vecchia, they passed by an unfamiliar place filled with big ugly rocks. The mud was deep, and the horse, driven by the drunken man, was running wild with the buggy lurching from side to side. *Oooh, oooh, oooh*, the sound of the heavy current of the river paralyzed Papà, and he thought to himself, "The buggy will turn over and we'll end up in the river and die!" He laid his head on his cousin, and eventually, when they reached a dangerous spot by the river, *Mbe-te-bum, Mbe-te-bum*, the buggy turned over and he landed on top of Guglielmina. Terrified, he hugged her so tightly that he couldn't breathe—and she was screaming because she had broken her leg. Taken by horse to the nearest hospital in Pratella, the trip was agony for Guglielmina. The pain, the river, the drunken man, and the mud that was taller than the horse's legs. In a whisper to himself, Papà thanked God that he hadn't been injured.

48

The bond between my papà and his cousin was so close that, many years ago, when Papà was in Vairano on vacation, she went to visit him and didn't want to let him go. Papà loves to tell us that the drunken man leading the horse looked as dangerous as the river, and that he had a thick black mustache that went all the way down to the sides of his mouth, where he puffed on a wooden pipe. Papà says, "It was like being in a cowboy Western, except it was real life!" Papà often identifies with the adventures of movie characters. He knows how to tell a story and can still leave me spellbound.

Chapter 8

MAMMUCCÈLLA'S CHILDHOOD

After her fragile beginning, Rosa grew strong and showed remarkable spirit. She was the child who always volunteered to help with chores or run errands. Her easygoing personality made her as obedient as her favorite sheep, Bianca. Well-loved at home and throughout the village for her enthusiastic, helpful nature, Rosa was never idle and made life easier for her older sister, Deméneca, and younger sister, 'Ndenièlla, dialect for Domenica and Antonia, who were more rebellious. Whenever Nonna called out for help, 'Ndenièlla claimed to be busy sweeping her room and Deméneca grabbed the spade and said, "I'm already busy; I have work in the garden." Rosa's clever sisters managed to escape Nonna's demands, especially Deméneca, who was often seen only at mealtime, when she, as the eldest, had to serve the dinner. Everyone sat at the table while Deméneca filled one plate at a time and served each person their meal. But always, she served herself first, placing her full plate on top of *la matarca*[19] until she was ready to sit down.

One day, Deméneca was asked to fetch a bucket of water about two blocks away near *ru férrar* (dialect for *il fabbro*, the blacksmith), where water surged from a big hole in the ground and you could easily fill your bucket. She was making *la vrénna* (dialect for *crusca*, a mixture of the residue flour from grinding wheat and hot water, used to feed the pigs). Deméneca didn't want to go, so she coaxed Rosa, who was only seven, with a promise to make her a rag doll if she went in her place. Excited, Rosa took off like a missile with the bucket, but while she was running, she tripped and fell on rough cobblestones and began bleeding profusely from her forehead. A neighbor, nicknamed Zi Maria de Meschelétta, saw her and quickly brought Rosa into her house and wrapped a towel around her forehead while someone else ran to tell Nonna.

---

19. Dialect for *madia*, a large wooden cupboard that opens from the top, traditionally used in rural houses, with a small window at the bottom where maize easily flowed out as needed.

In those days, due to lack of medical care, the villagers used ancient remedies passed down from their ancestors. Nonna burned scraps of *cannavo*, dialect for a hemp material grown and made in Gallo, which she collected from used tablecloths, ropes, nightgowns, and bed sheets. Every day, the ashes were soaked in olive oil to make a paste, and this remedy was put on Rosa's wound and covered with a handkerchief three times a day for a month. To this day, Rosa has a smooth diagonal scar over her left eyebrow and recalls, "It felt like *la ferita* [the wound] of Santa Rita, and I felt like a nun because, after the fall, my head was covered with a cloth."

From January to June, when the harvest was finished, families had to shop at one of the few *botteghe*[20] in the village. Nonna always shopped at Zia Catarina's bottega located uphill about two long blocks from her house. It was especially convenient, because Zia Catarina gave credit, recording unpaid purchases in a large debit book. Each August when Nonna received money from *ru staglie*, she would pay off her debt at the bottega. (*Ru staglie* is when you lease your own land and the profit from the produce grown on it gets divided in half between the owner and

20.   Plural for grocery store; *bottega* is singular.

the tenant.) Before leaving for America, my grandfather's brother, Benefàzie, bought land in Vairano Patenora with the intention of returning, but, when he decided to stay in America, he let his brother, my nonno, farm the land. This income helped my mother's family survive for many years until Benefàzie sponsored Giovanni, Nonna, and the children to join him. At that point, the land was sold to pay the passage for everyone but Rosa, who was the first to marry and start a family of her own.

Even as a small girl, Rosa was always different from her sisters. They never wanted to go to the bottega when Nonna asked, because they were ashamed of their poverty. It embarrassed them to have to purchase their food on credit, but Rosa was always happy to go. Nonna would say "She's like lightning," because Rosa would return so quickly with whatever was needed: *zucchare*[21] (sugar) or *uoglie*[22] (oil). She'd rush into the store and say, "Zi Catari, Mòma said to give me a kilo of *maccarùne* (pasta)" or whatever was needed in the house. One day when she asked for *re schiarfilicchi* (slippers) for her sister 'Ndenièlla, Zia Catarina replied, "But you're barefoot, so here's a pair for

21. Dialect for *zucchero*.
22. Dialect for *olio*.

you, too." And Rosa ran off as quickly as she had arrived, calling reassurances to Zia Catarina as she disappeared through the doorway: "Come August, Mòma's going to pay you back."

Her cheerful nature made Rosa everyone's favorite, especially Demìnecu, her maternal nonno, who returned home from the United States after suffering a brain injury when Rosa was three years old. Demìnecu would sit at the window where he loved to watch the rain, and he loved to play with Rosa and teach her things. For instance, one day, when he was holding a slice of bread that had holes in it, he sat Rosa on his lap and said, *"Resé, Resé, uàrda, uàrda."*[23] And then he held the bread up to the window and told her to look through it, saying in the familiar dialect, "Now you're going to see the transparency of the bread."

When she wasn't busy running errands, Rosa loved to play with her siblings and friends. Nonna made dolls out of kitchen towels, and all of her children and their friends played house. If it was nice outside, they outlined "houses" on the ground with pebbles that separated each house from its neighbor. One child was the mother, someone else the father (living in the same house), another was the sister

23. Dialect for "Rosa, Rosa, look, look."

or the aunt. The children became very excited protecting their "houses," yelling, "Don't come here! It's my house!" if anyone stepped even slightly over the pebbles. Even Zi Demìnecu (Rosa's brother, not to be confused with Nonno Demìnecu) would play house with his sisters.

As the only boy, Zi Demìnecu was treated special. A son, especially in that era, was considered to be a gift. The birth of a boy was a sign of power because it meant that the family name would live on. Males were the providers, while women took care of the home, so a son represented financial stability. This place of respect gave the men control of everything, and wives obeyed their orders, often catering to their every wish.

Zi Demìnecu was spoiled as a child and threw tantrums when he didn't get his way. Even outside in the street, he'd yell and carry on, and most of the time, a well-meaning neighbor would offer him biscotti. "Here is *re vescuòtte*;[24] just be a good boy," and as soon as he spied the sweet, he'd grab it and instantly forget the tantrum.

Rosa's childhood was spent in a house near the piazza, and on summer evenings, she loved to go outside and play with the neighborhood children. When the stars came out,

24.   Dialect for a *biscotto*, a kind of cookie

the children would hold hands and skip in a circle, singing at the top of their lungs, *"Ecco la luna, ecco le stelle, ecco gli angeli con le bellelle."*[25] In the daytime, when Rosa wasn't busy doing chores, she played with her friend Carmelina, who lived next door. They were so close that Rosa would eat at Carmelina's house one day, and the next day Carmelina would eat at Rosa's.

Every day before she grazed the sheep, Rosa had to feed the five chickens that lived in the stable with the sheep. On one wall of the barn was a wooden shelf where the chickens slept and laid their eggs. Rosa would run home from school, or interrupt her playing in the summertime, to tend the animals. The sheep started to bleat as soon as they heard her footsteps approaching, and, when she opened the door of the stable, they'd flock to her, eager to go outside. Rosa's grazing schedule was different from that of the other villagers because she was so busy, and she was often asked, "Resé, when do you graze your sheep?" because no one ever saw her. Rosa would reply, "At noontime," and they'd scold her saying, "You're going to let them die." Over time, as they saw Rosa bringing her

25.   "Here is the moon, here are the stars, here are the angels amidst the beauty."

sheep back home from grazing, they expressed surprise, saying, "*Caspita!* [Good Gracious!] Your sheep are nice and plump, and ours, grazing from morning until night, are so thin—you're a saint!"

As a child, Rosa became ill with a disease called *la nefrita*, nephritis, and her eyes and legs swelled up. Dottor Pilla, the town's only doctor, saw her and told Nonna that Rosa couldn't go outside, not even for fresh air, until she was fully recovered. One beautiful spring day, while Rosa was ill, she saw the splendor of the sun from her bedroom window and became hysterical because she wanted to go out and feed the chickens. When her mother left the room for a minute, Rosa took *la cavetta*,[26] an oval container or mess tin that Nonno had brought back from the military, filled it with *granone* (corn), and ran outside toward the chicken coop. It was about a block away from her house, and on the way, she met Dottor Pilla. Rosa greeted him enthusiastically—"*Buongiorno, Dottó!*"—and kept going. When she returned home, she announced proudly, "Mò, guess who I met on my way to feed the chickens? Dottor Pilla!"

Her mother answered anxiously, "*Tu me fai i 'ngalèra*," meaning "You're going to get me put in jail." At that

26.   Dialect for *gavétta*.

moment, there was a knock on the door and it was Dottor Pilla. He said, "Maria, what did you do? You made Rosa go out!"

She said, "Dottó, she went out while I was in the other room. I didn't see her."

So the doctor said, "Well, if she doesn't get sick from going out this time, she'll be okay. So tomorrow, if she hasn't relapsed, let her go outside."

Dottor Pilla was married to a woman named Tina, and they had a son named Ettoro. Not a Gallese, Tina came from a nearby town, and she spent all her time by the window at her sewing machine. She was thought of as strange because she never went out, and the only time the villagers saw her was when they went to see the doctor, because his office was in his home. From time to time, when neighbors came to see the doctor, Tina would say, "*Uàrda mó ve facce vedé na cosa,*" or "Look, I'm going to show you something." And she would touch something under the sewing machine table, and the sewing machine would start walking around the house by itself. The story goes that they called her *La Fantasma*[27] *of Dottor Pilla* because she could make the sewing machine table chase people,

27. Phantom.

especially if she knew they didn't like her or that she was the subject of their gossip, and she only did this when her husband wasn't at home. The villagers were frightened and told Dottor Pilla, but he reassured them, "My wife likes to kid around." But the neighbors stayed away unless they had to see the doctor.

Chapter 9

MAMMUCCÈLLA AND WORLD WAR II

It was the end of March, beginning of April 1940. Mòma was only three years old, but she always remembered the earsplitting explosions—*bum! bum! bum!*—that woke her in the middle of the night. Immediately, the whole village ran into the streets, where they saw huge fires on top of the mountain, L'Acchia della Macchia. Everyone remained outside for fear their houses would be bombed. Soon it was announced that the *Tedeschi* (Germans) had attacked in the mountains of Gallo. By morning, a German troop had spread into the town, entering home after home in search of food. They turned the villagers' houses upside down and opened the matarcas, taking whatever food they found. Pointing their guns, they threatened to kill anyone who refused. The troop set up camp in Zia Catarina's bottega because it was well stocked with food, and threw her and her family onto the street. Soldiers roamed the village, breaking into homes and stables, stealing chickens and pigs, killing them for food, and leaving behind any part of the animal they didn't like. Frightened, all the villagers fled to the mountains and *grottas* (caves), wherever they could find a place to hide.

Nonna refused to leave. When the soldiers arrived at her door, she was ready for them. Sizing up the situation, she had already sent her husband, Giovanni, who wasn't as shrewd, to find refuge at the Falascóse, a far-off mountain where they owned some land that had a crumbling grotta he'd often used as shelter when it rained. Nonna's attitude was, *I want to see what these soldiers are going to do.*

At the time, the family lived at Via Piazza, near the main church, and Nonna left their door wide open after purposely messing up the house. Beds were unmade, with pillows, sheets, and blankets thrown on the floor, and she waited with her four small children by her side. The lower part of the house was a stable for the *ciucciariéglie* (donkey) they needed to go to the mountains. She hid him behind the *catassa*, a fake wall she made by stacking firewood in front of him, leaving a barely visible *senghetèlla* (space) just

62

large enough to slip food through. Nonna told the donkey, *"Te sò messa l'acqua, i te porte a magniò l'èreva tutte re iurne; tu n'alluccuò, sennò re Tedeschi te se pigliane i t'accidene,"* which translates to "I gave you water and I'll bring you grass every day; don't you scream or the Germans will take you and kill you." This intelligent donkey remained so still, she could barely hear him breathe.

The stable had only a small square window in the front and looked totally abandoned. When the Germans peeked in the window, Nonna said, *"No agline, no ova!"*—"No chickens, no eggs!" Then she grabbed her four children and invited the soldiers inside the house. Picking up a piece of stale bread, she said, *"Veléte magniò? Do you want to eat?"* The soldiers said no and gestured that she should feed her children instead. They never returned, but other homes that had been well stocked were completely ravaged.

Rosa's hair was blond when she was a child, and the family teased her. "You'd better be careful. The Germans might think you're one of them." She wasn't allowed outside during the Nazi occupation, so she would stand in the doorway, tall like a soldier, with her hands at her sides, imagining that she was protecting her family. Rosa also pleaded with Nonna to let her go out, saying, *"Mò,* they're not going to do anything to me." However, her older sister, Deméneca, was so terrified that she never left the house and hid under the bed whenever soldiers were nearby, especially after any particularly horrific incident. For instance, one time, a young man from the village, wearing American clothes he had gotten from his relatives abroad, was killed on sight because he was assumed to be a spy.

After the Allied troops successfully drove the Axis forces out of Sicily, the Allies continued traveling north to invade the mainland. Disembarking in Salerno to fierce resistance, they moved on to Naples in pursuit of the German Army. The Germans fought the Allies' advance to Rome by setting up a series of defensive lines, but the Allies infiltrated the mountains in pursuit of the German forces and dismantled the defensive lines, clearing the way toward Rome for the liberation of Italy. This challenge was more difficult than anticipated due in part to the terrain: "Eight hundred miles long, it was the most vertebrate of countries, with a mountainous spine and bony ribs."[28] Facing unexpected hardships of weather, rough terrain

28. Atkinson, Rick. *The Day of Battle: The War in Sicily and Italy, 1943-44* (The Liberation Trilogy Volume Two) (pp. 180-181) Henry Holt and Company, 2007.

and resistance from the enemy, "Italy would break their backs, their bones, and nearly their spirits. But first it would break their hearts, and that heartbreak began north of the Volturno, where the terrain steepened, the weather worsened, and the enemy stiffened."[29]

In the fall of 1943, American troops arrived in Capriati a Volturno, which was twenty minutes away by car. They set up camp, and a battalion was sent into the mountains of Gallo to look for Nazis.[30] However, unknown to the Americans, German soldiers with machine guns were still hiding in the area and shot and killed many of the young Americans. Even though their fleeing meant the end of the Nazis in the area, it was a time of deep sadness. After the tragedy, according to the villagers who were present, Don Michele rang the church bells, 'ndon 'ndan, 'ndon, 'ndan, to honor the dead. The priest then went up to the mountains

29. Atkinson, Rick. The Day of Battle: *The War in Sicily and Italy, 1943-44* (The Liberation Trilogy Volume Two) (p. 251) Henry Holt and Company, 2007.
30. For a fuller description of Gallo Matese during the 1943 campaign, see Chapter 2, "Across the Matese Mountains Valle Agricola, Letino, and Gallo, October 26–November 3, 1943" in Van Lunteren, Frank. *Spearhead of the Fifth Army: The 504th Parachute Infantry Regiment in Italy, from the Winter Line to Anzio.* Havertown, PA: Casemate Publishing, 2016.

to bless the slain GIs and say mass. All the villagers accompanied him and grieved to see so many dead bodies. The men of Gallo and the neighboring village, Letino, carried every soldier down the mountain and placed his body in a coffin. The coffins were left in the mortuary, which was next to the cemetery, and the United States was informed.

Through stone pines and flame-shaped cypresses they trudged, past farm cottages with chimneys poking like snorkels above the red tile roofs. Peasants keened over their dead, or rummaged through their ruined crofts to salvage a copper pot or a rag doll.[31] This description of the rugged corridor of the Upper Volturno, fall 1943, evokes the haunting effects of WW II in the mountains of central-southern Italy.

For a couple of weeks after this episode, American troops came into Gallo by truck every day for several hours. They set up alongside re Ponte (the river), where they built a fire and cooked food in a huge *quavédare*[32] and served all the villagers, who brought containers from home. Afterwards, they drove up to 'Ngòppa a ru Còlle and parked their trucks on the street in an open area next to the nursery

31. Atkinson, Rick. The Day of Battle: *The War in Sicily and Italy, 1943-44* (The Liberation Trilogy Volume Two) (p. 257) Henry Holt and Company, 2007.
32. Dialect for a round black cauldron lined with copper.

school, where they gave out handfuls of American candies to the children. Word got around, and Zia Deméneca came out from under her bed carrying her sister 'Ndenièlla on her back, and Rosa followed, all of them excited to receive candy. Children came running, and whenever adults joined in, the soldiers yelled, "Only children!"

Rosa loved the Americans. Seeing that her dress was ragged and torn, they gave her one made of camouflage material that looked like an army dress. She wore it all the time. One day when she was at the barn feeding the chickens, a big truck filled with soldiers passed by and Rosa called out, *"Buongiorno, Buongiorno!"* They threw her a big box of American crackers, but Annélla de Papalétta, a thirteen-year-old neighbor who was watching, grabbed them away from her. Seeing this, one of the soldiers jumped from the jeep like the devil and ran after Annélla. With nowhere to escape, she got scared and started climbing up a wall, but she got stuck with her legs dangling. Seeing the soldier behind her, Annélla threw him the crackers, and he returned them to Rosa along with an extra box, a bar of soap, and another dress made from beige corduroy. *"Grazie, grazie,"* said Rosa as she ran home.

This was a dark period of great famine in Gallo, with no food, clothes, shoes, detergent, or medicine. The

Germans had emptied Zia Caterina's bottega, and Zia Mariannina's bottega was still in town but had hardly any produce, and no one had money to shop. Some villagers had crops from the mountains, but others did not. Nonna had nothing to feed her children. Desperate, she made *re frattàcce*,[33] cornmeal with la vrénna, which is usually given to the pigs. She also went into the fields with a knife and cut wild chicory to cook.

American soldiers went through the village knocking on people's houses to see what they needed. Speaking only English, they gesticulated with their hands—for instance, putting their fingers in their wide-open mouths to ask if people were hungry. When they arrived at Nonna's door and saw her four children, they gave each one a box of crackers. Then Nonna made them understand that she had nothing to feed her children, and if they could give her more, she would give them a sheep. They came back in a truck filled with cases of crackers and gave them all to Nonna. Then one of the soldiers carried the sheep away draped over his shoulders like a collar.

Everyone was hungry, so when Rosa's neighbors saw

33. *Frattàcce* is a hard polenta that is sliced and eaten with cooked greens and beans, a recipe characteristic of Gallo Matese.

all the crackers, they ran over saying, "Lucky you!" and Nonna was happy to share them.

The American soldiers were generous, but the food shortage was greater. In Capriati, they had tents filled with supplies, such as canned beans, Spam, and crackers. So the young women of Gallo grouped together and walked to Capriati to get food. Being surrounded by so many handsome young men, the women became intoxicated and made up a second stanza to a popular song, *"La Molisana"*:

> *Discendi dal Matese la Molisana[34] la Molisana*
> *Ha negli occhi l'ardor*
> *Sulla bocca l'amor*
>
> *Le paesane nostre*
> *Son facce toste 2x*
> *Nel vedere di arrivar*
> *C'e speranza di sposar*

34. Females native to the Molise region, the border of the Matese Mountains.

Translation:

> *Descending from the Matese the Molisana the Molisana*
> *With ardor in her eyes*
> *And love on her lips*
>
> *Our countrywomen*
> *Are very daring*
> *With this arrival*
> *There is hope for marriage*

Many of these young women stayed behind in Capriati. Some got pregnant, but a couple of them were fortunate enough to have the soldiers fall in love with them. These soldiers went to speak with the women's parents, and, when it came time for them to leave, they took their Italian girlfriends to America. There they married, had children, and later came back to visit, further cementing Gallo's ties with the United States.

Three years after the war, a surprising thing happened. When Rosa was eleven years old, she and her friend Deméneca went with her aunt, Zia 'Ngelélla, to graze their sheep at L'Acchia della Macchia, the mountain at the Valletónna. While the sheep were grazing, Rosa found some unusual bones. She told the others, and they began to look around. Soon one of her friends found human skulls. They rushed home and told their parents, and it wasn't long before word spread throughout the village, even to the mayor. It was decided that the children had found the remains of soldiers from the war, so Don Michele went to bless the bones, and a mass was said before they were buried on the mountain. From that day on, the mountain was called *La Montagna Salera, The Salty Mountain*, because it was believed that the decayed human flesh from the bones made the ground salty.

Chapter 10

MAMMUCCÈLLA GOES TO THE CONVENT

When I think of my mòma, I think of a holy figure, a Madonna whose love for God is infinite, eternal. This is how she appears to me, and, as I've learned my mòma's story, I realize that her love of God was central long before I was born. When Rosa was ten years old, she attended Catechism classes, *la Léttrina*,[35] and in August 1947, she made her First Communion and Confirmation. In those days, these religious milestones, observed more simply than they are today, were done together. The children attended classes for a shorter period of time, and there was no celebration or special dress for the occasion. Even without

35.   Dialect for Catechism.

a lot of festivity, Rosa took these religious practices and sacraments seriously, and, on her first confession the day before her First Communion, she went to the church by herself and walked up to the priest and told him, "Don Michele, I want to confess."

He replied, "Come here and kneel down, my child."

Rosa knelt in the middle of the church where there were other people praying, and the priest asked, "What's wrong? What sins do you have?"

"I said *no* to Mòma."

"That's okay. Go and say three Ave Marias to La Madonnina," and off she went.

From that time on, Rosa always preferred to speak face-to-face with the priest, and never felt a need for the privacy of the confessional when confiding her sins. She felt completely at home in the church and was always comfortable with the priest and nuns. Recently, in talking about her early years, she confided, "The priest and nuns were everything to me."

By the time she was eleven, boys already admired Rosa, and the most ardent was Domenico. On a beautiful sunny day in June, Mòma was heading toward the mountains to graze her sheep when she heard Domenico, a wealthy boy from the village whose family owned lots of land and animals, call to her, "Resé, Resé, come and graze your sheep here in my parents' field so we can play hide-and-seek."

She enjoyed Domenico's company without ever thinking he had a romantic attachment to her. Frequently, after that, she would go to his private field where his family's cows munched on the grass as her sheep grazed, and she and Domenico had plenty of opportunities to run and play. It came as a complete surprise to Rosa when one day Domenico announced confidently, "I want to marry you when you get older," and she quickly gave him a firm, "No, I want to be a nun."

Shocked, he replied, "Are you crazy? Why, why, why?" and he became hysterical crying. The more Rosa said, "But that's what I want," the more he cried.

By 1949 and her twelfth birthday, Rosa's calling to become a nun was all-consuming, and she confided her wish to the Mother Superior, Suora Bernadetta, who then had the task of telling Nonna, who was not happy with the news. This caused Suora Bernadetta to enlist the town's well-liked priest, Don Michele, to help Nonna accept the idea, and it worked. Shortly after, it was decided that Rosa would leave her home and go to live with the nuns in the convent to begin her training. In the early morning darkness the day she was to leave, Rosa kissed all five sheep and they answered, *bè-è-è, bè-è*.... She then somberly kissed her siblings goodbye and set out accompanied by her parents, Suora Bernadetta, and Don Michele to catch the five a.m. bus that would take her to the convent of the Suore Immacolatine at Massa Lubrense in the province of Napoli.

At the last minute, feeling himself deeply in love, young Domenico appeared by Rosa's side begging her not to leave. As the bus arrived, he lowered his head and mumbled, *"Arrivederci,"* and then watched Rosa, her mother, her father, Zio Giuseppe, Suora Bernadetta, and Don Michele board the bus and ride away.

There was no direct bus from Gallo Matese, so they took the local bus to Caserta, where they caught a bus that went to Massa Lubrense, the town in Napoli where the convent was located, in the district of Monticchio. Filled with excitement, Rosa felt the ride went quickly, and before she knew it, she was scooped into Don Michele's arms and carried swiftly up the steps and over the threshold into the convent, where he announced enthusiastically, "Look, I'm bringing you a beautiful *bambina!*"

Residents of the convent Suore Immacolatine consisted of the teaching nuns, postulants, novices, and new arrivals. The Mother Superior and older nuns lived in another building in the town of Massa Lubrense near the Church of the Suore Immacolatine. As soon as Rosa entered her new home, she was welcomed by clapping hands and a song of goodbye to her family, because now her love was to be Jesus. While everyone was singing, Suora Giuseppina Cacace, Mother Superior, presented Rosa with a bouquet of mixed flowers—roses, carnations, and daisies. It was already late, so when the song ended, it was time for dinner.

After a full-course meal, Rosa calmly said goodbye to her family and followed Mother Superior to her new room, which, because she was so young, she had to share with Suora Eduardina, who was thirty years old.

Rosa was to be a postulant for three years, and since everyone had chores to do, she felt right at home. One week she was assisting in the kitchen, another she had to sweep the long hallway and all ten dormitories. Rosa took to the routine right away, and soon her responsibilities increased. One Thursday, Suora Giuseppina took her into Massa Lubrense to shop and meet Salvatore, the butcher. After this, every Thursday morning, Rosa went by foot through a shortcut in the mountains to buy chopped meat and cutlets for the week, accompanied by Annuccia, an eight-year-old orphan. It was a long walk, but Rosa loved the outdoors.

As soon as she entered the butcher shop on her first day, Salvatore asked, "Are you the new arrival? What do you want? What did Mother Superior tell you?"

Rosa promptly responded, "Three pounds of chopped meat and four pounds of cutlets. Mother Superior will come and pay you."

"*Si, bimba mia*, yes, my child, I'll give you everything right away."

While he worked, Salvatore inquired, "Where did you come from, *bella*?"

Always happy to talk to people, Rosa, an animated conversationalist, fired back, "I come from Gallo Matese!"

When her package was ready, Salvatore patted her on the head, saying, "Go ahead, go slowly, and give my regards to Mother Superior. I'll see you next week."

"*Arrivederci, arrivederci. Grazie, Salvatore.*"

During the three years of postulant training, Rosa had the same routine.

This was the daily schedule at the convent:

5 a.m.	Morning bell
6–7 a.m.	Prayers in the *Coro* (choir room)
7–8 a.m.	Mass in the chapel
8–9 a.m.	Breakfast in the refectory

9–noon	Chores
12–1 p.m.	Lunch in the refectory
1–2 p.m.	Prayer and Litany to the Madonna (in hallway outside the refectory), and then rest in her room (except when assigned to the kitchen)
2–3 p.m.	Finish chores
3–4 p.m.	Prayers in the *Coro*
4–5 p.m.	Recreation (piano lessons, singing, talking, and games)
5–6 p.m.	Personal tasks in the oratory (darning, mending, embroidery)
6–7 p.m.	Prayer and recitation from *L'ufficio* (sacred book) in the *Coro*
7–8 p.m.	Dinner in the refectory
8–9 p.m.	Meeting with all the nuns and recitation of evening prayers
9 p.m.	Bed

While she did her chores, Rosa always sang softly to herself the song she'd heard the shepherds at home sing, *"La mamma di Rosina era gelosa, bim, bum, bam."* Eventually, another postulant overheard her. She liked the song and told the Mother Superior, "Rosa sings a good song while she sweeps," asking, "Can she sing it to us at lunchtime?" From that day on, at every lunch, Rosa sang the song while everyone in the dining room accompanied her by banging on the tables and joining in on the chorus.

Rosa loved poetry as much as singing. During her first year, she was the youngest postulant and was chosen to learn a beautiful poem, *"Sbocciare di Fiori D'Anime,"*[36] to recite for Mother Superior's birthday. One afternoon, Rosa went into the empty kitchen to get some bread. Another postulant named Giulia Mozzone snuck in after her, grabbed a large knife, and screamed as she came toward Rosa, "I've got to kill you because you know everything!" Fortunately, a nun heard her from the hallway and came running in to stop her. She took the girl to Mother Superior, where it was learned she was jealous that Rosa could sing the Antiphona and the Oremus in Latin, and she couldn't, no matter how hard she tried. Fear of the girl's instability led to Giulia's being immediately expelled.

After completing three years as a postulant and three years as a novice, Rosa became a nun and her name became Suora Maria Rosaria. As a nun, she was transferred to a

36. "Souls Blossom Like Flowers."

small town called Maddaloni,[37] where she worked with other nuns to care for 300 children attending l'asilo (nursery school). She enjoyed teaching them poems, as well as songs, numbers, and the rosary.

My mother's faith was unshakable. From the time she arrived, nothing tempted her away from the convent. For instance, even at fifteen, when she was finishing her postulancy and Domenico, her childhood friend, appeared at the convent to plead with her to come home and marry him, she told him, "This is where I belong." He was leaving for Argentina, where he expected to find better work, but before he left he had to try one more time with Rosa. After Rosa confirmed that she was happy in the convent, Domenico left for Argentina and was never heard from again.

After a year and a half as a nun working successfully with the children, Rosa's duties were increased. She was assigned extra chores, a few of which were disagreeable to her. Although she felt they compromised her integrity, she remained silent and obeyed. But her internal conflict was further fueled when she had a misunderstanding

37. It is in the province of Caserta, and the town of Maddaloni is linked to the city of Caserta.

with the Mother Superior that left her humiliated. Uncharacteristically, she went to her room in tears.

As she sobbed, she was startled by a knock on her door. It was her parents surprising her with a visit. In a vulnerable state, she sank into her mother's arms, crying. Seeing her daughter so upset angered Nonna, who immediately demanded, "What are you doing here? Why don't you come home!"

Nearly hysterical, Rosa replied, "Mò, I really want to come home."

This set in motion a three-month process, which Rosa came to regret but over which she had no control, especially when, after the order's first refusal, Nonna threatened to burn down the convent.

Chapter II

MAMMUCCÈLLA
BACK IN GALLO

Back home in Gallo, Rosa felt strange and missed the convent, but did not believe, even for a minute, that she would never return. Now nineteen years old, her work in the household was much as it had been before she left—cooking, cleaning, washing clothes at the fountain, and running errands. But there was one important change that deepened her sadness: the sheep were gone. Her brother, Demìnecu, who had been assigned Rosa's job tending the flock when she left, had rebelled. He did not like being a shepherd, so one day he threw a couple of sheep off a cliff. Nonna got the message and sold the rest, including Bianca, Rosa's favorite. Losing this part of her routine made her even more disoriented to be away from the religious structure of the convent, where she had tended children instead of sheep.

It didn't take long for Rosa to be noticed by the boys, but this scared her because she saw the world outside the convent as full of sinners. To Rosa, even kissing was a sin. Whenever she saw a boy she knew was interested in her, she would change her path. One day, she rode the donkey to L'Acchia della Macchia to bring her father empty burlap sacks for the corn he was harvesting. After Nonno filled the sacks, he loaded them onto the donkey so Rosa could carry them home. On her way, a handsome villager traveling in the opposite direction approached. He said, *"Signorina, ti devo dire una preghiera,"* (Miss, I have a prayer I want to tell you.)

In her naïveté, his meaning escaped Rosa. She did not understand that she was the prayer and he wanted her. Instead, she took him literally and thought he had a prayer for her, a prayer he wanted to teach her. She responded enthusiastically, "Oh, yes. It's nearly one o'clock; let's go to church and say a beautiful prayer." She was excited because, in the convent, everyone prayed the litany after lunch. Her mind was always filled with the spiritual, and she was confused when the boy laughed and replied, "That's okay, I'll have you speak with my sister, Maria, tomorrow."

Later in the day, Nonno unpacked the corn from the sacks and Rosa helped him shuck the ears before placing them in the sun to dry. After a day of hard work, Rosa went to bed early, forgetting about the boy she had met on the path until the next day when Maria appeared. What a surprise it was for her to hear the stranger's sister explain, "My brother likes you and wants to propose marriage." So, that's how it came to be that Rosa rejected another suitor.

Corn was a staple of the peasant diet, primarily prepared as polenta or frattàcce. The process of making the corn into grain took some time. Once the ears were dry, the corn was hit with a wooden pole until all the kernels fell to the ground, where they were gathered and put into a sieve to shake off the dust. The maize was then placed on top of a sheet spread out in the sun where it could dry completely. Later, it was put into buckets and poured carefully into la matarca for storage. As needed, maize was taken to the mill to be ground into flour, and going to *re muline*[38] was Rosa's job. But here, too, she encountered challenges.

When she made her first trip to re muline after returning from the convent, the owner said, "*Come sei bella signorina*— You're a beautiful young woman," as he caressed her arm.

38. The mill.

She replied, *"Si guarda con gl'occhi e non si tocca con le mani*—Look with your eyes but don't touch with your hands!" and was startled when he snapped back, *"Vedere e non toccare e una cosa da crepare!*—To look and not touch will make me explode!"

Clever at dodging unwanted attention, Rosa smiled, *"Crepate!* So explode!"

In no time at all, Rosa got into the rhythm of the household and was as eager as ever to be useful. For example, when Nonna had to go with 'Ndenièlla, one of Rosa's younger sisters, to stay in a relative's house in Vairano while getting treatments for her eczema, Rosa traveled back and forth from Gallo to Vairano to bring them supplies. There was always a strong connection in the family between the two towns, so Rosa enjoyed making the trip. She traveled by donkey, always with another female villager, taking the shortest route through mountain paths. They would leave at nine in the morning, arrive in Vairano at three in the afternoon, and stay in Vairano for a few days before returning home.

My mother's family knew many Vairanesi, including my father's family. Therefore, it was not at all unusual when Ituccia, my father's cousin, asked Nonno if she and her baby could stay at the house one night when she came to

Gallo. Ituccia and her infant were traveling to Gallo with my father (who had just lost his mother in Vairano) to introduce him to a prospective wife recommended by a relative. For this trip to Gallo, Antonio was given a place to sleep at the girl's house, but there wasn't enough room for Ituccia, so she and the baby stayed at Rosa's. However, when Ituccia returned home to Vairano, she realized that she had left her baby's blanket back in Gallo. Fortunately, Nonna happened to be in Vairano, so Ituccia asked her for help. Nonna reassured her that Rosa would soon be coming to Vairano with supplies. This is how my mother happened to meet my father when she carried the baby's blanket with her to Vairano and went to Ituccia's house to return it. Antonio, who had not liked the other woman in Gallo, fell instantly in love when he saw Rosa.

Nothing was said to Rosa, however. Instead, Ituccia and Zia Annetèlla, Antonio's aunt, went to Nonna, who then relayed Antonio's interest to Rosa, who did not want to get married. Still devout and wishing she could return to the convent, Rosa's life revolved around the liturgical calendar.

Disappointed, Nonna tried to talk sense to Rosa. She explained that she was lucky he was from a good family, that marriage was expected, and that it was dangerous for her to remain single. Nonna lived in fear that Rosa would be taken advantage of, or worse, become pregnant. She pleaded with her to consider the offer, and finally Rosa's resolve weakened and she said, "I'll think about it."

The pressure did not stop there, because Antonio's father and aunt also came to speak with Rosa on his behalf. In turmoil, Rosa decided to talk to the priest at Vairano. He confirmed that Antonio came from a good family. The priest also asked, "What do you desire?" and Rosa answered, "To lead a holy life." But she was influenced by his response: "My dear child, being a mother is more saintly than being a nun."

Eventually, to obey her parents, feeling sympathy for Antonio, and trusting the priest, Rosa reluctantly agreed to marry Antonio in Gallo. But when Don Michele was told, he wasn't pleased that Rosa was to marry a stranger from another town. Her priest since childhood, and the one who had brought her to the convent, Don Michele was very protective.

Finally, unbeknownst to Rosa, Nonna solved the problem by getting two false testimonies from a wealthy Gallese family who lived and owned factories in Caianello, a nearby town, saying that they knew Antonio. The wedding day was set for January 24, 1959, three months after their initial meeting. During the exchange of vows, Don Michele lowered his spectacles and looked Rosa straight in the eye. "Rosa, do you take Antonio to be your husband?"

She felt as if the priest's eyes penetrated her soul. Frightened, she whispered, "*Sì.*"

Chapter 12

ROSA D'AREZZO
AS A NEWLYWED

Antonio's family was still in mourning for his mother, so after the ceremony in Gallo, there was only a small celebration back in Vairano at his father's house. While the bride and groom ate a home-cooked meal with their family, a townsperson played a few songs on the *organetto*.[39]

The sacred sacrament of marriage still placed great importance on the bride's virginity in the 1950s, even though the means of verification had become less direct. After their first night together, spent in the upstairs loft of Nonno Bartolomeo's home, Antonio's sister, 'Ngiulinèlla, served them breakfast in bed. At the same

39. Accordion.

time, she changed the sheets.

The adjustment to marriage was not easy for Rosa. She was used to warmth and affection, but Antonio was not demonstrative. He never expressed feelings, but she knew he worried about making a living. Their first home together was in Vairano with his family. Jobs were scarce everywhere in Italy, so he traveled to nearby towns wherever there was work. Transportation was difficult, because at that time, there were no buses, so he rode a *mòtom*, a small, inexpensive moped that did not need a license plate. Whenever it broke down, he had to walk for long hours to and from wherever he could find work, often returning home late at night. This is why Nonno Bartolomeo bought him a Lambrètta 150,[40] a more powerful bike that sat two. In the meantime, Rosa took care of the household and got to know life in a larger town, where, in those days, pregnancy was expected to happen shortly after marriage.

When Rosa didn't become pregnant right away, she went to the doctor. He put her on a treatment that consisted of a syrup containing nutrients and fifteen injections of vitamin B12. It worked, because the next month she became

40. Commercial name for a motor scooter put out by the company Innocenti.

pregnant. In the fall, with a baby expected in March, the couple anticipated their need for more space and hoped to find a place of their own. Once again, Nonna came to the rescue and made arrangements with a neighbor, Maria de re Liégge, who was emigrating to Argentina and offered Rosa the use of her house for as long as she wanted it. The house was located near Nonna's, on Via Piana, otherwise known in dialect as *sótte a la Vachiòna*, which means "down to the flat plain." Her new home consisted of only one room with a rough cement floor, and, like all houses in the village, it had no bathroom, running water, heat, stove, refrigerator, or telephone, but Rosa was grateful for Signora Maria's generosity and felt blessed.

There was no hospital in Gallo, and Dottor Pilla was the only doctor, so all babies were born at home with the help of family and neighbors. Dottor Pilla was present for Rosa's first birth and was assisted by Nonna and Zia Matalena, dialect for Maddalena. Embarrassment at having her body exposed and worry that people would hear her scream was the hardest part for Rosa. She began to cry, holding the sheet in her mouth so no one would hear. Fortunately, the birth went well and the newborn, me, was named Angela after my father's deceased mother. I was called Angelina by my parents and in Gallo, 'Ngelé by everyone else. According to Mòma, I slept through my first month of life. She believed this was normal for all babies "then, but now infants are born intellectual and with their eyes open."

In our village, it was the custom that, with the first child, a new mother would receive a visit every day for forty days from a woman named Zia Annélla de Masciéglie. Dottor Pilla had trained her to assist with births and with caring for newborns. This custom was common in Italy, especially in villages without hospitals, and is perhaps the origin of doulas,[41] a service that is increasingly popular in the United States today.

Zia Annélla taught my mother the art of swaddling still practiced in Gallo when I was born. Just like all the babies in my family who preceded me, I was wrapped every day from my shoulders to my toes, with only my face showing, until I could walk. Each time Mòma unwrapped me to change my cloth diaper, she felt as if I was a newborn chick breaking free of its shell, with arms and legs stretching like wings. Between Zia Annélla and Mòma, I

41. A woman trained to give nonmedical assistance to a woman in labor, and to provide emotional and physical support throughout the childbirth process.

received meticulous care, but so did Mòma. It was an old Italian myth that for the first two months after childbirth the lactating mother had to be fed a special broth. Daily, Zia Matalena and Nonna took care of Mòma. They would kill a chicken and feed her the fresh chicken soup with pastina and two eggs beaten into it to increase lactation and make her body strong.

My name, Angela, means "messenger of God." I would have preferred to be named after Venus, the goddess of love, since I admire beauty, attractiveness, and almost everything that is sensual. Now I think maybe God did want me to be his messenger instead.

Chapter 13

ANGELA'S EARLY YEARS

The 1950s continued to be a dark period in Gallo, as southern Italy struggled to recover from the war. Many men had to leave their families behind to earn a living. They relocated to countries such as America, Canada, Australia, Venezuela, and Argentina, anyplace there was work.

This meant that more and more farms were abandoned. By 1960, when I was born, opportunities for employment were developing in northern Italy, with the start of Fiat (which is an acronym for Fabbrica Italiana Automobili Torino) and Alfa Romeo production. These car companies created 30,000 jobs, causing many others from the south to relocate to Torino and Milano. Unable to move his family anywhere, my father, through a friend's connection, found work in Zermatt, Switzerland, coming home once or twice a year to see us. This is how I came to be alone with Mòma for the first two years of my life.

Papò wrote letters and sent money but he had not seen me since I was six months old. When I turned two, Mòma sent him my photograph, and shortly afterwards, he returned to Gallo, appearing at the front gate like a stranger. I began to cry hysterically when he tried to pick me up, and I clung desperately to Mòma. In time, I got used to him, and to this day, my mother believes, "If it wasn't for your photograph, I don't know if he would ever have come home." After this visit with Papò, Mòma got pregnant with my sister Maria. This was the pattern in those early years, especially because there was no contraception. Every time Papò came home, Mòma got pregnant. With my father away so much, it is no wonder that my earliest bond was with my mother.

There was a time when all newborns in Gallo wore a red ribbon tied in a bow and pinned to the left side of their chest. This was a poor man's substitute for the small golden horn or a religious medal pinned to the clothes of babies in wealthier towns to protect them from the evil eye. It was believed that wearing a gold horn or a religious medal would deflect evil spirits away from the baby. Red ribbons were endowed with the same power—the bright color would draw attention away from the baby, and the person casting an evil spell would look at the ribbon before the infant. By the time I got to l'asilo, the nursery school, a small religious medal of La Madonna di Montevergine pinned to my underwear replaced the red ribbon. I loved l'asilo, which was located at ru Còlle, an area on the outskirts of the village. It was run by nuns and was spacious, with a large terrace where we used to play. Even though it was called the nursery school, l'asilo was really a day-care center for children two years old and up.

Breastfed until I was two years old, I was nursed only twice a day from eight months, when I started on soft food. Mòma has fond memories of this time, at *mieze iurne*, noon, when the sound of the church bells signaled her to feed me *pon cuótt*, a dish commonly fed to babies in Gallo Matese. Pon cuótt is made from leftover hard bread soaked in boiling water with oil and a little salt until the bread becomes mushy like a pudding. Afterwards, she would take me for a *passeggiata*, a stroll around the neighborhood, and buy me a *pastetta*.[42] Satisfied, we'd return home, where I was

42. Dialect for biscotto, an Italian cookie.

content to play.

The only exception to this routine was during the first summer after Nonna's departure for the United States, when I was about six months old, and Mòma had to go to the Valletónna to tend the grain Nonna had sown before leaving. My mother's friend and neighbor, Zia Capóne, came with us, and Mòma carried me all the way on her head in a wooden cradle. When we arrived at the field, she placed me on the grass under a shady bush, where I played on a blanket until lunchtime, when Zia and Mòma would join me for a picnic. In the afternoon, I napped in my cradle with a white mesh veil draped over it to prevent mosquito bites while Mòma worked. One day, Mòma came over to check on me and I started crying because I didn't want her to go. She said, "Don't cry, let me take care of the land," and I startled her by saying my first sentence as clear as a bell: "Mò, let Zia take care of the land; you take care of me."

My constant companion was *la pupélla*, a cloth doll Mòma had made for me. I played with la pupélla in the *loggia*, the little fenced yard in front of the house, and would place her in *la cónnola*, the cradle, and rock her saying, "*La pupélla stó dermènne*, the doll is sleeping." Mòma would put her index finger by her lips and say, "Sssssssst, don't make any noise or she'll wake up," and for a while I would play quietly with small rocks, making houses.

Good at keeping me entertained, Mòma and I sometimes played with water in front of the house. She would fill *la cunchetèlla* (a small pot), and I would blow into *re scisciatùre*, a heavy wrought-iron flute-like pipe used to start the fire in the fireplace by blowing on the coals. It had two holes in the bottom and a large hole at the top. When I blew in it, the water inside would make bubbles, and the *cuà, cuà, cuà* sounded like a duck. If I got bored, Mòma would take me inside to make pon cuótt. Then, I would get *la pupélla* and feed her pon cuótt, just as Mòma had fed me, holding a spoon to the doll's mouth, dirtying the bib, and then *tac, tac, tac*, I would tap her back the way Mòma had taught me. Of course, Mòma always got stuck washing the doll's dirty bib.

Luckily, by the time I was born, women didn't have to go to the river to do their wash because Gallo had a fresh-water fountain made for scrubbing clothes, and it was near our house. Women filled their barrels, buckets, or *cónca* (large pots) and carried them home on their heads. Every day in the early afternoon, Mòma rocked me to sleep in a wooden cradle so she could go and fetch the day's water and wash my dirty diapers. According to her, one day, while rocking me to sleep, she sang a unique Gallese lullaby about *melélle*, small apples.

> *Zitte patróne mi mògna melélle,*
> *stasera ce ne iamme cu le stélle*
> *lè lè lè lè*

Hearing the song, I began to cry frantically, demanding, "*No lè lè lè*, I want *le melélle*."

Mòma kept singing and trying to calm me down:

> *Zitte patróne mi mògna melùne,*
> *Stasera ce ne iamme cu la luna*
> *lè lè lè lè*

Even when she sang the second verse, which was about melons, I kept crying for apples, so Mòma took me into town to buy me apples. That was the end of that song and the beginning of a new lullaby in two verses by the Bulgarian poet Petko R. Slavejkov, sung in the Gallese version.

Verse One:

> *Fatte ne suónne ca Maria mó passa*
> *Porta ne gigli mmane i a tè re lassa*
> *Fatte nu suónne ca Maria è passata*
> *ne giglie mmane a tè te rè lassàte.*[43]

Verse Two:

> *Hanna Madonna mia vestuta ianca*
> *A chistu figl levace ru piant.*

> *Hanna Madonna mia vestuta nera*
> *A chistu figl levace le pene.*

> *Hanna Madonna mia vestuta roscia*
> *A chistu figl levace la tossa*

As I got older, the lullabies were replaced by fairytales like *Pinocchio*, *Cenerentola*,[44] and *Cappuccetto Rosso*,[45] and since there were no books available, Mòma would repeat them

43. These lyrics are as I remember them and as they are written in Pasqualina DiLullo Iannitti's book, *Gallo Matese: Sul Filo della Memoria*, p. 72.
44. *Cinderella.*
45. *Little Red Riding Hood.*

over and over again. I felt protected as I listened intently, enveloped by the warm presence of Mòma, who never left my side until I was asleep. Later, when it was her bedtime, she would climb quietly in beside me, as Papà was usually away.

We remained in Gallo long enough for my sister, Maria, to be born, when I was three. My memories of Maria's birth are vivid but mixed. All the attention was upstairs in Mòma's bedroom, and I was left alone in the loggia for what seemed like an eternity. I don't remember exactly how it happened, but I must have been bored and started playing with a button on a sweater that my mother had left lying on top of the stone wall. The next thing I remember is that I had trouble breathing. Somehow, the button had come off the sweater and wound up in my left nostril. When Zia Rosa de Tirr-tigl finally came to check on me, she said, "Angelina, what are you doing?"

I pointed to my nose. She looked and saw the button way up into the septum. She panicked, smacked me, and called for her mother-in-law, Zia Maria, and her sister, Zia 'Ndiniillétta, to come down right away. Zia Maria told me to blow my nose hard, but I didn't know how and inhaled instead, causing the button to travel even farther up. The poor woman quickly removed a bobby pin from her bun and shaped it into a hook that she tried to insert into my nostril. Even though Zia Rosa held my head and Zia 'Ndiniillétta my legs, I wasn't staying still. Zia Rosa smacked me again, but even so, Zia Maria was unsuccessful. I can still hear her urging me loudly, "Angelina, blow, blow!" but I inhaled. Her anxiety was visible and I got scared. Somehow, out of nowhere, I finally figured out how to exhale through my nose. I blew hard and out came the button!

Left alone again, my next memory is of Zia Rosa hollering out the window, "It's a baby girl!"

Another story from when I was three involved money. Papà got into the habit of giving me ten lire once in a while, but not to spend; I just liked to hold onto it. One day, I was outside playing in the loggia and overheard my parents arguing about not having any bread. My mother was upset. So, ten lire in hand, I walked on my own around the corner to the grocer, 'Ndònio de Scudìglie, and asked him for a loaf of bread. When I arrived home and happily presented the bread, my parents were even more shocked than the grocer had been. They hadn't even realized I was gone. Later, my mother ran to the grocer and explained. To this day, my mother can't understand how, at three, I picked up the urgency of their conversation and took it upon myself to solve the problem.

From my earliest years, observing and then doing was my forte. Always at Mòma's side, I watched with amazement how she blew re scisciatùre to start the fire and pleaded with her to let me try. As soon as the embers were glowing red-hot, she'd hand the flute-shaped pipe to me. The first few times, I inhaled instead of blowing, and the ashes went into my throat and made me cough. Determined, I kept at it and finally succeeded.

Mòma kept me occupied. I helped her pick up le ceppetèlle, or dead branches, from the lane leading to our house. She was also full of simple surprises, like burying an unpeeled potato under the fire's ashes to cook. When she pulled it out and removed the skin, we shared the unexpected delicacy of a roasted potato that seemed to appear like magic.

My love of nature must have started early, when I was living in Nonna's house in Gallo, because to this day, I have vivid memories of being small and playing in the surrounding gardens. To the left coming out of Nonna's door, there was a chicken coop with four chickens. One of my first household chores was to feed the chickens and see if there was an egg to add to my pastina for lunch. I would holler out, "Mò, Mò, there's an egg!" Mòma would come outside, grab my hand, and we would go together and retrieve the prize.

A low cement wall separated the loggia from the garden, and, with my pupélla, I could play there happily alone, nourished by air made sweet from trees and bushes laden with fruit and roses. Entering the house from outside, I delighted in passing through the dangling multicolored plastic strips hanging from the doorframe in the summer to keep out flies. Indoors, I was Mòma's shadow while she did her chores. Even today, she'll say, "You were glued to my leg like a magnet." Now I realize how precious that time alone with her was.

When I was four, Mòma taught me a poem dedicated to fathers, which she had learned in the convent in preparation to be a teacher:

> *Son piccina*
> *Son carina*
> *Son la gioia di papà*
> *Se mi sporco la vestina*
> *E papà mi batterà*

Translation:

> *I'm tiny*
> *I'm cute*
> *I'm daddy's little joy*
> *If I get my dress all dirty*
> *Daddy will paddle me*

Mòma would make me stand in the middle of the house, with my short dress showing my chubby legs and ruffled underwear, and have me recite the poem to Papò while he wig-wagged my hands in gestures that went with the poem. Papò would pick me up, hug me tightly, and say, "*Sta spusélla mia*, my little bride." This expression was common in Vairano at the time. It did not mean an actual bride, but that a little child was associated with a bride because of the intensity of the love.

I definitely have some of my father's traits. He has always been very theatrical, exuberant, entertaining. Once, when I was about three and Papò was home from Switzerland, a photographer came to Gallo from Caianello, a small town twenty-three miles away—one hour by car through the mountains. We did not have any cameras, so the only way people could get photos of their loved ones was when, every so often, a traveling photographer came through town. Mòma asked Signore Camerata to take a family photo of the three of us. Papò was holding me in his arms for the photo when Zia Rosa brought over some freshly made biscotti. Papò quickly grabbed one and placed it on my arm like a bracelet, and the picture was taken.

A year later, when Mòma became pregnant with her third child, my sister Rita, Papò came back from Switzerland, speaking fluent French, and decided to remain in his homeland. He moved us back to his native town, Vairano, where he had an opportunity to get work. In fact, that year, forty-eight families from Gallo moved to Vairano because there was less famine there. The Vairanesi called the people from Gallo *gli scarpìtte* because they wore *re scarpùne*.[46] In Vairano, everyone wore shoes, so when they saw a villager from Gallo, they would say, "Look, look, *gli scarpìtte* are coming."[47] The Gallese would fire right back, "*Scarpe massicce i cerviéglie fine*," which meant "thick shoes but sharp brain."

As I remember it, just because we moved to Vairano, things didn't really calm down. After we got settled, Zi

46.   A local peasant footwear, no longer in existence, with soles made from rubber tires, that looked like canoes with holes for black leather laces that tied halfway up the leg.
47.   An insult that refers to Gallese peasant footwear, *scarpùne*.

Peppino, nicknamed, Furficcióne, meaning "big scissors," who was the husband of my father's sister, Zia 'Ngiulinèlla, informed Papò that the carabinieri were in the new section of Vairano and on their way up to where we lived in il borgo to draft him for the military. Immediately, my father took off, leaving all of us, and ran to Mount Pièsco, where he hid behind a tree. He'd had just enough time to tell Mòma to go downtown to the new Vairano and inform Ettoro, one of his friends who had a car, to meet him at a familiar place with his passport and a small piece of luggage, and off he went to Switzerland again. At the time, it was obligatory for men to serve in the military for at least four years, but as the breadwinner of the family, Papò was deeply frightened and chose to leave Vairano instead. When he found out that it was safe to come back, he returned home. Papò is a character. If he'd only had the opportunity to study, he would have been outstanding in the arts of comedy, music, and theater. He's just a passionate, naturally funny man.

With the birth of my sister Rita when I was five, the tradition of naming children after relatives was broken, as the name Rita was my father's choice. He was working in the town of Cassino, making mattresses from *la sdramma*,[48] and he liked the name of his boss's daughter, which was also the name of a famous Italian singer, Rita Pavone.

Meanwhile, in September 1966, I started first grade in Vairano, but by the following January, when I was halfway through second grade, we returned to Gallo, where my mother had my brother Claudio. This is where we stayed until I was ten and we left for the United States. My brother is named after Claudio Villa, a famous singer at the time. It doesn't surprise me, knowing the passion my papà has for music. I still remember Papà's melodic singing along with Claudio Villa's favorite hits, like "O Sole Mio," "Granada," and "Chitarra Romana."

---

48. Vairanese dialect for a wild grass once used to make mattresses. The Latin name is *ampelodesmos mauritanica*.

Chapter 14

PAPÀ'S FEAST DAY AND OTHER FESTIVALS

My father loves to tell stories about the feast day of San Bartolomeo in Vairano, which was celebrated on August 24th. The festival went on for three days, and the town hired a troupe of folk dancers and musicians dressed in native costumes. One of the dancers led the procession, carrying a pole seven to eight meters high, with fifteen colored ribbons hanging from the top, each held by a dancer. When the music started, the dancers began to entwine the multicolored ribbons around the pole, so that at the end of the procession, the pole was encased in ribbons neatly woven from top to bottom.

The *Masti di feste*[49] had approval from city hall to collect money from each person in town to organize the feast. Therefore, they rotated the event site yearly to keep everyone happy, and to ensure future donations, they were careful to let different areas host the event. The feast that my papà and his friends remember most was held at *piazzale*[50] Mannurito. There were activities such as *tiro alla fune*, or tug-of-war, and *la corsa nel sacco*, or sack race. The hardest game, and my papà's favorite, was a competition to climb a ten-meter pole, made slippery with soap, that had prizes like panettone, liquor, bread, and money at the top. One by one, men took turns trying to reach a prize. Slipping off over and over again, they had to go to the end of the line and wait for another turn. It wasn't until all the soap was worn away that climbers reached the top. This sacred festival is still celebrated but has been modernized to include elaborate lights and bands from nearby cities.

When I was a teenager, I learned my papà had a secret. I had always known that my nonno, his father, was named Bartolomeo, and that my father's name was Antonio, or Tony (as he renamed himself in America). But what I had

49. Master of feasts.
50. Small piazza.

never known was that he'd already changed his name once before. Having been born on August 24th, Papà had been given the middle name of Bartolomeo, a name he refused.

In the 1950s, on summer Wednesdays, a flea market (*mercato*) took place in the middle of La Piazza di San Giovanni in Vairano. Vendors came from nearby areas such as Caserta, Napoli, Isernia, Venafro, and Campobasso, and sold American clothes, picture frames, chickens, and all kinds of other items.

The flea market filled the piazza with townspeople browsing, buying, or just taking in the colorful sights, meeting with neighbors, sharing a word or two, and enjoying the summer weather.

My papà at age fifteen had the same curiosity he has now for anything that is a bit different. As a teenager, he loved venturing into the flea market with his eyes wide open. Now, his favorite and most vivid memory is of a zodiac fortune-telling *pappagallo* (parrot) with green, pink, and white feathers, sitting in a painted cage. A small table was in front of it, level with the cage, and on the table was a wooden box aligned with the door of the cage. On top of the wooden box, within easy reach of the pappagallo, were many folded notes (*bigliettini*) for all the months of the year. These notes held the mystery of your fortune, based on your astrological sign and the pappagallo's intuition.

According to Papà, the pappagallo was a trained fortuneteller who could intuit people's fortunes by reading their energy and selecting the appropriate fortune for them from among the zodiac bigliettini. Customers first had to speak with the owner, who always stood near the cage. You had to pay five lire to the owner and tell him your birthday—month, day, and year—and then he would instruct the pappagallo to tell your fortune. The wise pappagallo then studied your face, and, when ready, he slowly and with great deliberation picked up a bigliettino just for you personally and gave it to his owner. The owner always read the fortune out loud, since many people did not know how to read at that time.

Waiting for the pappagallo to choose your fortune generated heart-pumping excitement, and opening the note felt metaphoric because it contained your future, and, as my father says, everyone knows that if your belief in something is strong enough, it will happen. According to my father, the fortunes chosen by the pappagallo did happen. His approach was in strong contrast to the beliefs of my mother, who, at age fifteen, was living in a convent where she put all her faith in God.

Chapter 15

LA LAMBRÈTTA

Even though my memories of Gallo are strongest because we spent more time there, much of it when I was older, I do recall strong images of living in my father's village. Our house in Vairano Patenora was down the road from the Piazza Mannurito, and because there was no running water, the small fountain located in the piazza was the hub of all Vairano's activity. Daily, women took turns scrubbing dirty clothes on laundry boards that they carried on their heads from home in large cunchelìnas.

The fountain was a gathering place where the towns-people stopped to splash fresh water on their faces to cool off or to drink it with their hands, while others filled jugs to take home. Here people greeted each other, talked, and caught up on the news. Often, if my mother wanted to clean the house, she would leave me with my younger sisters at the fountain with a friend who was doing her wash, and we would play outside while the friend kept an eye on us.

Recently, enjoying pastries with our coffee and talking about our experiences in Vairano, my mother and I laughed harder than we had in years. Her cheeks reddened and her eyes glistened. In this moment, my mammuccèlla did not seem old-fashioned or from another generation's culture. The lines of worry were gone from around her eyes until her face suddenly darkened and she asked me, "Do you remember the motor scooter?"

I was about five, and we were living at Via San Tommaso, in il borgo of Vairano, less than a block away from Mannurito, in a small house that my paternal grandfather, Bartolomeo, had bought and given to my parents because we were too crowded all living in his house. He paid mille lire for the house. At that time, this amount was equivalent to one dollar of American money, and in Italy, you could feed your entire family for a week on mille lire. I clearly remember living in that house and my mammuccèlla's calling it *la baràcca*, meaning a hut, because it looked like an abandoned house. It was one big room with a roughly finished *astreco-grézzo* (cement) floor and a half wall that divided the room into areas for a kitchen and a bedroom. La baràcca was dimly lit with two bare light bulbs overhead of no more than forty watts each— you could barely see your own feet. It was as if we lived in a tavern.

There were no bathrooms or running water inside any of the houses where we lived. With no toilets, people used the woods or an abandoned house, cleaning themselves with leaves, grass, rags, or whatever they could find at home like an old newspaper. Our water for cooking and washing came from the fountain of Mannurito, and before the fountain was built, everyone carried their water from the Fiume Volturno (Volturno River) outside of town, which bordered the territories of Ailano and Pratella, one and a half miles from Vairano.

During the winter, the kitchen fireplace kept our house warm and provided my mother a place to cook our meals. The problem was that it was illegal to chop down trees on Mount Catrèula,[51] so you had to buy the wood, but it was too expensive for people living in the old section of town. So at midnight, our families took their chances eluding the

51.   Dialect for Mount Cajevola.

patrol. On occasion, someone would get caught and sent to jail—like my aunt, who spent a few months behind bars with her newborn baby because of a firewood violation. In the summer, my mother used a *bibigas*, a small tabletop stove with four burners heated by a *bombola*,[52] and, when the bombola was empty, she called the vendor to replace it for mille lire, the same price as our house.

With only one bedroom, there was not enough space for three children, so I slept with Mammuccèlla during the week when Papà was traveling to Cassino for work. For six years, Papà slept at home only one night a week. On those nights, I slept at the foot of their bed in a cot with my sister Maria, and when Rita was an infant, she slept in a cradle on my mother's side of the bed. This was before the birth of my brother, Claudio.

In this new house, I missed *la paparella*, the duck that was at my grandfather Bartolomeo and Zio Alfredo's. She used to run with her wings up in the air, squawking, *cuà, cuà, cuà*, before settling down. Then I would resume playing under the fig tree with my cousin Lucio, who was eight years old when I was born and lived nearby. He would pick me up and spin me around until I yelled, "Stop!" And

52. Gas cylinder.

then I would beg him to do it again. In the late afternoon, Lucio and his friends often played cards at a table under the tree. They were always kind to me, never getting mad when I bothered them. They were playful and amused me with funny sounds and faces, and I would run away and then return, and Lucio would sit me on his knee. From my perch, I would watch the game. I had no interest in the cards, but I loved being with my cousin. Lucio's aunt raised him because his family had so many children. He had an identical twin brother named Mario who lived a few miles away with the rest of his siblings and their mother.

Next door to our new house lived Zia Rusina, a woman in her sixties with salt-and-pepper hair pulled back in a bun. The red beads she always wore around her neck looked beautiful to me against the black of her dresses. I can still visualize Zia Rusina because she resembled my favorite artist, Georgia O'Keeffe. They both wore black, with their hair pulled back, and both had a taste for striking colors. Zia Rusì's house had a small entrance in the bottom of the door for her gray cat. Whenever Zia Rusì saw us, she handed out chestnuts, so every day my sister Rita would go look for her, calling, *"Zesì, Zesì, le catagne*—chestnuts," and if she hadn't gotten dressed or was busy, Zia Rusì would hand Rita chestnuts through the little cat door.

My sister Maria loved another neighbor, Zia Carmela, who lived a bit farther up the hill toward Mannurito. One day, Maria disappeared, and my mammuccèlla panicked and ran first to Zia Rusì's and then to all the nearby neighbors, but Maria was not to be found until Mamma went up the hill to Zia Carmela's house, where Maria was happily eating grapes.

The Piazza Mannurito was one of the most beautiful areas in Vairano Patenora because it was full of olive trees. It had rock formations so huge they could only be removed with explosives. When I was very young, before the fountain was built, the women had no place to gather outside, but the men gathered by the olive trees and played *il gioco delle bocce* (bocce ball). The game was played in the open space in front of the church, and always during the day, since at nighttime, there were no lights. The winner was rewarded with Birra Peroni, the famous Italian beer, or *vino di uva fragola*, wine from sweet grapes grown in the vineyard. In my memory, everything there was scattered—dirt, grass, rocks, men sitting on the ground playing cards smoking Alfa cigarettes and flicking the ashes and butts as far as they would go. Their voices grew louder and louder as their excitement with the game grew, and anyone within hearing distance would know who won or lost. All the children played *la ciulélla*, Gallese dialect for an Italian version of blind man's bluff, or *buongiòsso*, dialect for our hide-and-seek. I remember peeking around the olive trees to see if anyone was hiding there. I'd say, "*Cìcì, cùcù,*" and, whenever I caught someone, "*Cùcù sette,*" dialect for "peek-a-boo" and "boo, boo, I got you."

The day that stands out most was the day I was finally allowed to go outside alone, after pleading with my mother, who was too busy to take me. My father was with my Zio Alfredo at the piazza, and Mòma weakened, thinking, *Your papà will watch you.* Delighted, I ran to Mannurito wearing my new butterfly dress that had just been made with fabric my nonna had sent from America. It was pink and covered with blue, white, and yellow butterflies, and Mammuccèlla had tied my hair up in *la coda alla gigliòla*[53] with a white ribbon. She remembers watching my chubby legs running in little black shoes so fast up the cobblestone road to join my friends playing hide-and-seek.

As I was running to hide behind an olive tree, I stepped off the cobblestones and felt a sudden pull on my dress that threw me up in the air. The next thing I knew, the front tire of la Lambrètta I hadn't seen coming had landed

53.   Half donkey tail (or ponytail).

on my left leg. I was crying, and my friends ran to call Papà, who was on his way home with Zio Alfredo. Hearing what had happened, he ran and gathered me in his arms and carried me home. When we reached our door, I fainted. Consequently, I didn't hear my mother's screaming when she became hysterical and lit into my father. Fortunately, the town doctor pronounced me fine, but the story is complicated.

It wasn't until recently that I found out what had really happened. That day, the motor scooter my grandfather, Bartolomeo, had given my papà as a gift to go back and forth to work, was parked by the church of Madonna di Loreto when Pascalino, his fifteen-year-old third-generation nephew, pleaded to take it on a short ride. Never in a million years did my papà imagine that Pascalino and la Lambrètta would wind up where I was playing. I never knew it was my father's Lambrètta that ran over my leg or that his third cousin was the driver. Nor did I realize all the facts behind my mother's hysteria that day and why she became so enraged at my papà.

The motor scooter episode has more poignancy in my imagination because Pascalino became ill and died at seventeen. This made me glad Papà had allowed him to take it for a ride, but when I asked him, "Why didn't you watch me?" he responded, "What did I know? I was doing my thing."

Chapter 16

THE ROMANI

One of my most vivid memories of Vairano Patenora is of the caravans gathered in a field with a group of Romani sitting in a circle. Their long, full skirts underneath aprons, colored kerchiefs tied on their heads, shawls over their shoulders, and large hoop earrings were so vibrant in the sun. No matter how many times I was told not to go near them, the Romani fascinated me. I was drawn to their clothes and their beauty, but most of all, like me, they seemed different and without a home in one place.

My papà says that, after World War II, the Romani migrated all over Europe, and their ancestors originally came from India. Their appearance was very different from what people were accustomed to seeing, traveling with their horses and wagons from town to town. People in our area were afraid of Romani and warned, "Stay away from them or they will kidnap you."

The Romani also had a reputation for being experienced thieves. My papà says, "You could be in the fields on a hot sunny day and one of the Romani would come and greet you with the most charming smile, talking sweetly while another Romani woman was stealing chickens. She would hide them under her skirt and take off while her friend was still talking." I also heard that the Romani used their skirts to carry knives that they wouldn't hesitate to use if you bothered them.

Now I understand that, for the Romani, it was an issue of survival. Years before they moved to Vairano, Romani had been persecuted and killed during World War II, just like the Jews, because of their beliefs and lifestyle. People wouldn't hire them in our area, so the Romani were impoverished and often forced to steal. They lived in squatter-like communities and were socially isolated from the people in town. The Romani were also known for their creativity and were famous for basket making, buying and selling animals, fortunetelling, and palm reading. They worked during the day, but at night, expressed their suffering through fiery dances, songs, hand clapping, and guitar music. The Romani culture is often credited with originating flamenco, even though Andalusia, in southern Spain, where flamenco flourished, is supposed to be its birthplace. The two main groups of Romani living in Italy are the Roma and the Sinti.

In the Italian culture, we danced *la tarantella*. Done with a partner, the women wear colorful, ruffled dresses with bright kerchiefs covering their hair. They shake tambourines above their heads as they circle their partners, or the couple grabs arms and spins right, then left. As a child, I danced la tarantella with my sisters, my father, and friends. We danced it in the house, on the patio, and at village celebrations. There was never a wedding without la tarantella. Maybe my earliest attraction to the Romani started because they reminded me of the thrill I had dancing to the intoxicating rhythms of the tarantella.

According to Papà, only about four Romani families lived in Vairano when he was growing up, but they did not do any stealing locally. Venafro, a subdivision of the city of Isernia in the Molise region, is where most of the Romani lived.[54]

---

51. Today in Venafro, there are communal buildings the town built to integrate the Italians and Romani, who still follow their traditions.

From there, they traveled with their horses and wagons to other towns, to beg or steal, or to sell their crafts so that they wouldn't starve. There were only about ten Romani families living in Venafro at the time, but the bulk of the Romani population resided in Isernia, side by side with the Italians. In fact, there were so many Romani in Isernia, the Vairanesi called it "the Romani city" or "*la mamma dei zingari*," the mother of Romani.

My papà has memories of a Romani family in Vairano with the Italian names of Pascaluccio and Giacomina and their son Miliano. They lived by a small piazza in upper Vairano called San Nicola, and when my father was a boy, he had to pass by their house every day on his way home from the fields. If he carried a big bunch of broccoli di rabe under his arms that he'd just picked, la Signora Giacomina would ask him to give her some. He told me, "She didn't bother anyone, and she was a nice woman, so I always gave her some." But, once he confided to me, "I was young, and, with all the rumors, I was afraid that if I didn't give her some, she might snatch them all." Today, la Signora Giacomina, her husband, Pascaluccio, and their son, Miliano, are all deceased. But Miliano's wife and children still reside in Vairano. His wife, 'Ndunetèlla, dialect for Antonietta, is an Italian woman, but even though she is not Romani, the stigma of being one is so strong that the townspeople call her children, the children of 'Ndunetèlla, la zingara.

There are many towns surrounding Vairano. The town of Ailano is located twelve kilometers to the northeast, and about eight more kilometers from Ailano, at the tip of a mountain, a tiny town grew up in a wooded valley called Valle Agricola, which is five kilometers from Gallo Matese going through mountain paths on foot or on horseback. For the Gallesi[55] and the Vairanesi, this town is known as La Vall. Surrounded by mountains, there was originally no land to cultivate there, but poor people flattened the rocky ground so they could build roads and houses, thus creating La Vall.[56] Years ago, all over Europe, food was taken by trailer to stores. But in rural mountainous areas like Valle Agricola and Gallo Matese, when snow and ice accumulated during months of bitter cold, the roads were so icy that helicopters were used to get food to stores so people wouldn't starve. My parents' towns, Vairano Patenora and Gallo Matese, were linked for many people, because the colder temperatures of the mountains in the north

55. People from Gallo Matese.
56. *Vall* means *valley* in dialect; *valle* is without dialect.

forced the Gallesi to rent stables in Vairano, where it was warmer and there was grass from November to March. This arrangement prevented their animals from dying of starvation, and before Easter, when the temperatures warmed and the grass was green, the animals were brought back to Gallo.

During the 1940s, a time of deep poverty throughout Italy, rural towns like La Vall and Gallo Matese were the poorest and most primitive. This meant that boundaries between who was a Romani and who was Italian could be unclear, because women from La Vall and Vairano and nearby towns still dressed in similar clothing to that worn by the Romani. For instance, my paternal grandmother, Angela, from Vairano, always wore a long dark skirt, earrings dangling from pierced ears, and a black kerchief on her head.

My mammuccèlla says that a woman from La Vall, accompanied by her husband, would come around to Gallo holding a wooden basket on her head filled with clothes to sell. Her husband would be shouting in the street, *"Maglie e mutandine from America*, T-shirts and panties from America," while his wife went door-to-door trying to make a sale. Eventually, she got to know people's names, and she'd say, "Zia Marì, do you want to buy a dress from America?"

This was typical for that small town, where goods unloaded from ships docked in Napoli found their way to the small villages. Bought or stolen, we never knew, but people did whatever they could to survive.

As a small child in Gallo Matese, my mammuccèlla tells me she remembers a woman from La Vall who went to her mother, my grandmother, Maria Cioffi, begging for food. My mammuccèlla thought she was Romani but says she could very well have been an Italian woman; there was no real way to tell. Pleading in the doorway, the woman would say, "Zia, give me something for the souls of your departed—I have *la cucchiarèlla*[57] to give to you." Nonna always gave her something—potatoes, bread, whatever she could spare—and, in return, she got a wooden spoon, very useful for stirring the red sauce or polenta. La Vall, because of its sweet wood, was the major town where all types of wooden kitchen utensils were made and then traded for food by the villagers.

Going from field to field, the Romani also dug up the white roots of a grass called *la ramégna*.[58] My papà was told as a child that it was used to make the most famous

57. Dialect for a wooden spoon that is a little larger than a tablespoon.
58. Dialect for la gramigna.

Italian beer, Birra Peroni, and that, once dried, the roots were gathered into bales and placed in caravans and brought to big cities like Caserta and Napoli to be sold to distributors. Recently, a friend from Vairano told me, "That's impossible. La ramégna was used to feed horses." To this day, it is a point of disagreement in my parents' home. Papà explains la ramégna with passion, saying, "It's like when you break in half the stem of certain flowers, or of a fig, a milky liquid comes out," and he adds, "In Vairano, only the Romani went into the fields to excavate la ramégna." According to him, the Romani who lived in more populated areas like Isernia and Venafro did not labor in fields, but made money buying animals and reselling them at la fièra.

Modern transportation didn't exist in Gallo Matese when I lived there, so the peasants who worked on farms used horses and ponies to get around. This meant that horses had an almost sacred importance. On farms, they were used for hauling and as a means of transportation for their owners. The area where I lived is called la Vachiòna, near the well where townspeople went throughout the day to get their water. Adjacent to the well was a tub of water where all the horses drank and were washed down after a day's work in the heat. The tub was the first stop the farmers made on their way home, and it delighted me as a child to see the horses jump in the tub and splash themselves. *Heeeeeeeeeeeeeh*, they would whinny exuberantly. With their big teeth showing, they seemed to smile as they dunked and then shook their heads up in the air, water dripping everywhere. A few steps away from the tub was a stone wall with four spouts of running water where women brought large pots and washed clothes. Before it was possible to wash clothes in town, women like my grandmother had to do their laundry in the river, *re Ponte*.

Sipping espresso in my apartment on a recent Sunday afternoon, my mother asked, "Did I tell you the story about the farmer and the horse?" As I shook my head, she continued:

"One day, a paisano complained that his horse was tired all the time and had no energy to work. He'd had the horse for many years, so he told his wife he was going to sell it at la fièra in a nearby town, where there were special days for selling animals. When the day came, he took his horse and sold it for thirty lire. Happy with the transaction, he went home to wait until the day for *buying* animals.

"That morning, he went off with confidence, eager to make a purchase. Soon, he stopped at the first merchant and said, 'I want a young, energetic horse.' The Romani said, 'No problem, I have a great horse for you,' and he smacked a horse on the rump. This made the horse rear up on his hind legs, and he looked beautiful. Nicely groomed, his mane was brushed aside so you could see his eyes, which appeared to gleam.

"The paisano fell in love and immediately paid the eighty-lire price and rushed home to show his wife. As he approached Gallo Matese, the paisano was amazed. 'Wow, this is such an intelligent horse, I don't even have to lead him.' Excited when he arrived back, he ran to call his wife, pulling her outside and saying, 'I bought the best horse there was!' A clever woman, she inspected the horse carefully and announced, 'You've been fooled. Can't you tell this is the same horse that you sold for thirty lire, cleaned up and fed, and now you bought it back for eighty?'

"He cursed, '*Porca miseria*, they tricked me!'"

Chapter 17

EARLY HISTORY OF GALLO MATESE

On a clear day, looking south from the mountains of Gallo, it is possible to admire the gulf of Naples and Mount Vesuvius. Napoli is the capital of the region, but the nearest large town, about seventy kilometers from Gallo, is Caserta. Modern Gallo has more roads making the mountain passes accessible, so it has become easy to visit nearby villages like Prata, Valle Agricola, and Fontegreca, places I never saw when I was a child. In fact, I never even went to Vallelunga, a village that belongs to the municipality of Gallo and is only six kilometers to the north.

Culture and tradition were so strong in the area that, despite their proximity, both villages had completely different ways of dressing. I remember being intrigued as a child hearing that the Vallelunga traditional dress was a long dark cotton skirt instead of Gallo's more provincial, shorter, heavy brown wool one-piece jumper (from the Bulgars), with thick white stockings. Once, I did go to Letino, a neighboring village in the southeast near the lake. I was with my father but don't recall anything except being amazed and feeling I was in another world. I've heard from my cousin Antonio that Letino now has a beauty salon where women from Gallo go to get their hair done.

In Gallo, all of our water originated in an area called Acqua Spruzzata, or spraying water, which flowed into the River Sava that fed the Lake of Gallo, fresh springs, streams, village fountains, and wells. Water from these sources was put into *la cónca*[59] or *barile*[60] and carried on the head, or by hand in *re cuate*,[61] all the way home. In the 1960s, no one in our village had indoor plumbing. I hadn't even heard of a toothbrush. Now we laugh when my mother describes her reaction when she first heard about oral hygiene in America and imagined a toothbrush as a broom for the teeth.

How Gallo got its name remains a mystery. It has been

59. Pot.
60. Barrel.
61. Bucket.

said that it came from the German word *Wald* (derived from the Latin word *gualdum*, pertaining to woods or forest), after Longobardo Wald, the German population that invaded Italy in the twelfth century. However, in Italian, *Gallo* means *rooster* (*gallus* in Latin) and most Gallese children grow up as I did, thinking that the town was named for the rooster. This belief is further confirmed by the town's coat of arms, which has two roosters and no forest. A legend that supports *rooster* as the origin of the name comes from our neighboring village. It is said that shepherds from Letino, hearing roosters from Gallo crow every morning, gave the village its name. Another complication is that our villagers speak dialect and call their town *ru Uall* instead of Gallo.

Unfortunately, after the 1860 unification of Italy, anarchist leaders had hopes of establishing a communal village with no ownership of property, and any documents that could prove and clarify the town's history were destroyed when rebel soldiers set fire to the town hall in 1877. What we know for sure is that the Romans called the inhabitants of this zone *Montesi*, habitants of mountains. There were many neighboring villages grouped together, all named after the mountainous chain connecting one to the other. Each separate village had a double name, with the second name being Matese, such as Piedimonte Matese, Castello del Matese, San Gregorio Matese, and Gallo Matese.

So, who were my ancestors? Many tribes lived in the Italian territory before the birth of Rome. The first settlers in the Campania Region were indigenous Italians of the south called Sanniti. A faction of the Sanniti, or Samnites, were an ancient, warlike tribe called Sanniti Prenti, who migrated up the mountainous chain of the Matese, where they lived in huts and some settled in Gallo. However, in that ancient time, Gallo was not a picturesque village. It was primitive and savage, with small swampy areas, fields, hills, and inaccessible mountains. The climate on the high plateau of the Matese had extra-snowy conditions lasting six months out of the year, and this harsh environment was a refuge for the Sanniti in their escape from Roman invasions.

After the fall of the Roman Empire, a Bulgarian tribe of shepherds, who were pure Tartars from Mongolia and led by Duke Alcek, left Asia in approximately 600 AD and crossed the Alps into Italy. Alcek allied with the Lombards and asked King Grimoaldo (Longobard) for land, along with permission to settle near Ravenna in northern Italy.

A few decades later, in 667 AD, Alcek made an agreement with Romualdo I, who was the Duke of Benevento in southern Italy and son of the king of northern Italy, to give him and his people several territories in the Campania and Molise regions. In return, Alcek had to give up his ducal title, disarm except to provide Romualdo I military service, and take up farming. Alcek was granted the Lombard title of Gastaldo (from Old High German), administrator of houses and land, similar functions to those of a mayor, thus uniting the Italian and Bulgarian populations. The Bulgars brought their technique of building houses using dry brickwork, or rocks without mortar, and with the Sanniti, they gradually created a village of this type of house in Gallo. These houses, from the Sannitic/Bulgarian time, were constructed with stairways to the second floor, almost always on the exterior, because families lived above their barns, which were used to keep animals and store produce such as grain, hay, vegetables, and prosciutto.

Mòma tells me that her maternal grandmother, Antonella, grew up in that type of house. She remembers the 1940s, when the stable was inside the house on the ground floor. The family used an outside staircase to get to their living quarters above the stable. She recalls that the family fed the animals by throwing hay down to the stable from upstairs, where there was a large square wooden door in the floor. When the door was closed, it was anchored shut by a hook. When the trapdoor was open, the hook was hung on the kitchen wall. Of course, by the time I was born, stables for animals were built separately, and people lived in the whole house.

We had a large kitchen downstairs, with a chimney and fireplace in the center. To the right as you entered the door was a brick oven, a table and chairs, and la matarca next to the bibìgas stove. There was a curtain underneath the brick oven where my mother sometimes hid a hen sitting on a basket of fertilized eggs in the warm darkness for forty days until they hatched. I loved seeing the little chicks break through the eggshells. In all the other houses in Gallo, families raised animals and hung sausages and joints of prosciutto from the ceiling to dry. My family was at a disadvantage because my father was not a farmer. He was from a non-farming family in Vairano, so we had no animals or produce, and our house did not have sausages and prosciutto. We only had chickens.

In medieval times, the Sannitis and Bulgarians joined in building the first church in Gallo, called San Simeone. The ancient church, long abandoned, still stands on ru Castellóne. Castaldo[62] was my maternal nonna's last name

62. From Middle English.

and the original surname of Gallo, which was derived from Alcek's title, Gastaldo. My connection to this history has become more important to me over time, and now it gives me a thrill to look up Gallo on the computer in my Manhattan apartment and read about things such as the elegant residence and office of my mother's doctor, Dottor Pilla, Il Palazzo dei Signori Boiani, a beautiful example of medieval architecture. The baronial palace was made of limestone and owned by a wealthy family from a nearby town. Today, it lies abandoned. I feel homesick reading about the main church of Gallo, Ave Gratia Plena, a medieval structure located in the piazza with a beautiful fountain, where I attended mass, Catechism classes, all the church activities, and festivals. I can still picture its baroque door and violin-shaped window.

Chapter 18

IL MALOCCHIO

Gallo Matese is so small that when I was young it did not even exist on most maps, and everyone believed in witchcraft, which they thought caused many illnesses and deaths. One such superstition is *il malocchio*, or the evil eye. The villagers believed il malocchio was the main cause of a headache or a stomachache, and came from someone's maliciously staring at you out of jealousy. Here is a typical conversation from my childhood:

"Mammuccè, my tummy hurts."

"Did anyone stare at you today?"

My mother actually knows which people to avoid because they are known for doing il malocchio. Until my teenage years, I wore a small pin of La Madonna di

Montevergine attached to my underwear for protection against the evil eye, but as I got older, I couldn't be bothered.

There is a ritual to remove the evil eye that my mother practices. She puts water in a pasta bowl, makes the sign of the cross, says the person's name and starts praying in a whisper. Then she dips her finger into some olive oil and shakes a few drops into the water, which causes a circular ripple. If the circles expand, it means you have il malocchio. The larger the circles and the more they expand, the more severe is il malocchio. For the ritual to work, the water must be left alone long enough for the circles to keep expanding and finally disappear. This way, the evil eye is removed. Even though the ritual is passed on from generation to generation, not everyone knows how to do it. My nonna taught my mother, and to this day, if the neighbors feel sick, they call my mother.

Moving from Gallo Matese to Little Italy in the Bronx when I was ten years old was like being in my small superstitious village, where everyone knew each other and news traveled fast. Until I was fifteen, my lifestyle had remained very European. For instance, after dinner my friends and I would go for una passeggiata, strolling up and down the neighborhood. We wore short skirts and giggled so the guys would notice us. One day, I noticed that the shape of my legs was a bit different from my friends', and it made me suspicious and embarrassed. I didn't want to wear short dresses anymore, but no one was aware of it except me, until one day I said, "Mammuccè, something is wrong with me—look, look how my legs are bulging."

My mother replied, "Angelina, there is nothing wrong with you."

But I was convinced that something was not quite right, and I pursued it with her because I wanted an answer. Finally, she acquiesced, saying, "*Domani*, tomorrow, I'll take you to Dr. Soscia."

Dr. Soscia didn't know what was wrong, so he referred us to a specialist. It took a year before I was finally diagnosed with muscular dystrophy. We did not know what that was.

As my disability progresses, I walk in the neighborhood holding onto my mother's arm. The news spreads fast, and neighbors give suggestions to my mother, who is in desperate need of a miraculous cure to heal me.

I am sent to an Italian woman in Queens called Mamma Marisa, who supposedly cures people. We walk into a big, mysterious house, and on top of her shiny cherry-wood furniture, I notice clear glass bottles with different designs inside. I am fascinated by a white ship inside one of the bottles, which is perfect and seems to be made of thin, white thread. Later, I learn that Mamma Marisa places egg whites inside bottles, and the shapes they take determine which remedy she is supposed to use. She charges my mother sixty dollars and asks us to return in a week, but I guess my mother's faith fails because we do not return.

A week later, we're at the bakery and a friend says, "Rosa, there is a woman in the neighborhood who does deep visualizations that heal people."

My mother replies, "*Mannaggia la miseria* (mild expletive), I don't speak English. Angelina, go knock on her door and find out when we can see her."

I had seen the woman in the neighborhood. She was thin, with long bleached-blond hair that she pushed up in a messy twist, and she wore heavy makeup, red, red, lipstick, and black tights. She was weird-looking. As I knock, I feel a spooky feeling creeping over me. Her husband opens the door, and he is wearing white long johns, looking as weird as his wife.

"I'd like an appointment with your wife," I tell him.

And he replies, "Come back tomorrow afternoon."

HELL, NO, I say to myself. I hurry home and never return.

A paisana named Giuseppina sees my mother at

church. "Rosa, I go to Dr. Marchetta, a chiropractor, and he is excellent. Why don't you take Angelina? Maybe he can help her."

So off we went to Dr. Marchetta. My mother was happy to know that he spoke Italian, not so perfectly, but they understood each other. When I first see him, Dr. Marchetta reminds me of St. Anthony. He has the same circle of baldness around his head, and his presence is soothing. On my first visit, he works on my body, bones, and muscles, cracks my neck, right to left, and cracks my back. I think my bones will break, but it feels good afterward. He finishes his treatment by placing his hands over my eyes without touching me. I close my eyes.

Dr. Marchetta asks, "Do you feel heat? Do you see colors?"

I shake my head no.

Then I hear a soft whisper as if Dr. Marchetta is praying, and I feel a burst of energy starting from my toes up to my calves. As he continues to move his hands over my stomach, he flicks them outward, *shhhh! shhhh!*

My mother tells me, "Angelina, he's getting rid of bad spirits."

With eyes still closed, I fall into a relaxing sleep...

After several sessions, I get the courage to peek, and

he is standing in the corner by the door with his eyes closed. After a while, he claps his hands, which means the treatment is over. It takes time, but eventually I am able to feel heat and see waves of purple and green during the treatments. That makes him happy. This is the way he ended every session.

After three years, Dr. Marchetta wants me to try one more thing. It is a Saturday in spring 1978, and I am now eighteen. Dr. Marchetta tells us about Father DiOrio, a famous charismatic priest with an ability to heal, who was touring California at the time.

He invites my parents and me to attend a religious retreat to see Father DiOrio when he comes to the New York area. My mother explains, "Angelina, it's because Dr. Marchetta wants to be one hundred percent sure that you don't have *la fattura*, a kind of witchcraft that the priest can undo, and you would be cured."

When we walk into the hall, I see two lines of women with chiffon scarves of different colors—purple, teal green, red, blue, orange—that they are waving in the air to the sounds of celestial music.

I say to my mother, "I'm scared, Mà. This is not Catholic."

The healing ceremony begins, it is my turn, and I

panic. Dr. Marchetta brings me into the middle of the hall. The priest places his hand on my forehead. As I drop to the floor, my eyes close. I hear voices, but I can't make out what they are saying.

"Get up."

"I can't."

"Don't say you can't, just do it."

I fake it, pulling myself up on Dr. Marchetta's arm. Everyone claps as if I'm healed. I know, my parents know, and Dr. Marchetta knows: no miracle happened.

In the car on the way home, my mother says, *"Figlia mia,* I thought you were dead! You were on the floor so long, and when they called you, you didn't move. Then I see Dr. Marchetta crying and I start to cry." She takes a breath, continues, "I wanted to touch you, but Dr. Marchetta said I should not cry or touch you, it will only be worse for my Angelina. And when you were asleep, twelve women circled you with open books, chanting, but you didn't get up when you were supposed to, so the women came back. I saw them chanting again, but they were circling you in the opposite direction. I think they were trying to reverse what they had done."

At my next treatment, I ask Dr. Marchetta, "What happened to my miracle?"

He pauses, pats my hands, looks me in the eye and says, "Angela, emotional healing is also a miracle."

The experience with Dr. Marchetta showed my mother that my illness was not *la fattura*. I was not under a spell. From that moment on, she knew only a scientific breakthrough would cure my muscular dystrophy.

And, now, many years later, my mother has found peace knowing that I am able to live on my own, and that if something happens to her, I will be okay.

Chapter 19

ZIA MATALENA

Everybody in Gallo knew each other by their sopranome (nickname). Ours was *Cap Rush,* meaning *redhead,* because my grandfather's brother, who moved to Argentina in his youth, had red hair. Zia Matalena, my grandfather Giovanni's half-sister, was called *Zia de Cinghiròna,* a family nickname that started long before she was born. Zia Matalena's great-grandfather used to say to his young son, "If you do these chores for me, I'll give you *cinque ròn,*" which is the equivalent of five cents. When it's said quickly, *cinque ròn* sounds like *cinghiròna,* so that's how this made-up word became the nickname for generations in her family, and my cousins Antonio, Giuseppe, and Franco are all called re figli de Matalena de Cinghiròna.

Zia Matalena's family lived by farming, and she was poor until she married Signor Antonio Mozzone, who returned from the war with tuberculosis. She was hired to take care of him, and they fell in love. Zia had always worn the costume of the town, but, with what seemed like the flick of a magic wand, Zio Mozzone turned the pumpkin into a princess, and she became the most stylish woman in Gallo. As a child, I always admired Zia, in her slim black skirt, just below the knee, knit shirt, styled hairdo like an actress from the '50s, and shoes with heels. Her hips swayed as she walked, and I imagined she was just like the famous Sophia Loren I had only heard about. Looking at Zia, you would never imagine she was the mother of three children, my cousins. Antonio, the oldest, was handsome and already studying to be a carabiniere in Caserta when I was a child, so I only played with Giuseppe and Franco. Summers, I had the time of my life at their house with so much open space.

You could see the lake from Zia's house, which was in an isolated area on the outskirts of town. They had only one neighbor, who lived way down the hill. In my childhood, none of the roads in Gallo were paved, and to get to Zia's secluded house, there was only a long, rocky lane leading to her front gate. First, visitors had to pass through a dark area that seemed to be an eternal tunnel with a floor of huge uneven rocks amidst tall trees that blocked the sky. I remember never wanting to go to Zia's on my own, for two equally terrifying reasons. There was a large hole in the rocks by the side of the road, where black-and-white vipers lived. I was told that if they bit me, I would die. One day, tiptoeing as I passed the snake cave on my way to Zia's, a huge viper suddenly appeared in the opening. It looked right at me, wiggling its long, thin tongue. I was terrified and stood still as a statue, barely breathing until the snake pulled back inside—and then I ran for my life.

The other reason I was afraid to go to Zia's, even when I wasn't alone, was that her neighbor had mystical powers. I don't even remember where I heard the stories, but it was known that this old woman could talk to birds. She would hold them in her hand and converse with them, and the birds would keep her informed about whatever she wanted to know. For instance, if she were curious about my home, she would assign a bird to follow her orders and bring back any information she wanted . Worse still, these birds were said to be people who had been her friends, and she had put a spell on them so they were loyal to her. We never saw this woman in town. I saw her only when I dared peek between the trees, and even though she was old and short with her hair in a bun like the other elders, she never wore the Gallo costume, and this in itself was strange.

The inside of Zia's home was more luxurious than everyone else's, except for the mayor and the doctor, because she had a sofa and a television, and outside, there was a large paved courtyard where my cousins and I loved to play, surrounded by hazelnut, fig, and plum trees. Next to the courtyard were stone steps that led up to a garden, which was protected by a black iron gate. The garden was off limits to children. Nobody but Zia was allowed to go inside. I still savor the sweet scents and images of her bending among the vegetables—basil, lettuce, cabbage, tomatoes, zucchini—as she picked them for our dinner.

Everything was heavenly there except for the worms, or *macciòlle*, squiggling on the ground, which grossed me out and made me scream. I was seven and played happily with my cousins, taking responsibility for my siblings. My brother, Claudio, was less than a year old, but I would sit him on their tricycle. It was the biggest thrill to be able to share my cousins' bike, since we didn't have one. I'd pedal as fast as I could, going in big circles, 'round and 'round, until I felt dizzy.

Playing outside was enchanting at Zia's house. Often, I'd stop what I was doing and just stare into the clear sky, and the sun was so strong that I had to lift my hand to my forehead to block its rays. The vast sky filled me with calm, a feeling of being alone in the blue space. Often during these interludes, I'd see a huge white bird with a large orange beak and a big pouch on its belly. Once, Mòma told me it was *la cicogna*, a stork, and the pouch was to carry newborn babies to their mothers. After that, whenever I saw a stork, I would ask, "Who's the baby for?" and my mother would answer with the name of a neighbor who was pregnant. This kept me believing, because, sure enough, the neighbor would have a baby.

Another excitement about going to Zia's house was its proximity to Il Lago di Gallo. We couldn't see the lake from my house, but the road to Zia's led to the lake, and it was exhilarating to look at its beauty from her yard. I never saw a soul there, except for the men who took care of the lake, an occasional boat, and swallows flying high above. This was before tourism caught on in Gallo. Now, people come from all over to picnic and enjoy its serene majesty. Growing up, I never knew the lake was an important energy source for the town. This makes me appreciate even more that Il Lago has remained unspoiled by industry and pollution. As Gallo became more modern, Zia's house remained untouched by time and progress, with its joints of prosciutto hanging from her ceiling and drinking water drawn from the well hidden behind the stairs that go up to the bedrooms.

Zia was devoted to her elderly mother, who lived with her. We called her Mamélla,[63] but her name was Catarina, and she stayed indoors except when we children teased her. Mischievous as we were, we loved to get Mamélla angry so we could hear her swear and gesture saying *"Vaffangulo,"*[64] waving her right hand madly in the air. It was exciting until Zia's authoritative voice would come to her rescue: *"Scite fòre, iate a pazziò*, go outside and play." Instantly, we'd all line up like a marching band and without a word or a glance head toward the playground. Despite our antics, it was a sad day for everyone when Mamélla passed away, as Zia's mother was the jewel of her home.

63. Old dialect for *grandmother*.
64. Dialect for "Go to hell."

Chapter 20

GETTING READY TO GO, MEDICAL CLEARANCE, AND SAYING GOODBYE

Zio Licandro, an independent agent who dealt with immigration papers, lived in a town named Ciorlano near Capriati, in the province of Caserta. He helped us get our papers together and set up necessary appointments, such as the medical clearance in Naples and the consulate.

My parents received the appointment for the medical clearance from the consulate in Naples through the mail. It was a special day for all of us. My mother dressed my sisters and me alike, in the same blue dresses we would wear again when we left for America, and she combed our hair in the same way. In my hometown, the hairstyle is called *la coda alla gigliòla*. It is a high ponytail made only with the sides and top of the hair while the hair in the back is left hanging long. Rita and I had bangs with that hairdo, but Maria's hair was too curly for bangs. We all had big blue ribbons tied in bows around our ponytails.

My sister Maria Domenica, who was seven years old and repeated everything she heard, said, "Mà, Mà, where are we going?"

"To Naples," my mom answered.

"We're going to Naples, we're going to Naples!"

I asked, "Mà, Mà, are we going to America?"

"No, we are going to Naples to see a doctor for medical clearance."

A doctor?

"Yes, a doctor."

I was delighted and stood by the door, ready to go to Naples.

My parents hoped that everyone would be okay and get clearance, but they worried because I had been going to doctors since I was a baby. At two and a half, parts of my face became jaundiced, especially around my eyes and along the sides near my ears. We were living in Vairano Patenora, my dad's hometown, when the doctor discovered that I had something wrong with my liver. The town doctor referred me to Dr. Visco, a pediatric specialist in Caianello, a nearby city. Dr. Visco referred me to Caserta, a neighboring city, for an X-ray to look at my liver. Dr. Visco called me Angelina, but to his staff I was *La Bella Bambina*. To this day, my mom talks about what a beautiful baby I was, and how, when they placed me on the stool to take the X-rays, I readily held my small arms straight ahead and didn't move until I was told. The results showed that my liver was not perfect, so the doctor gave my mother syrup for me as treatment. I returned to the doctor every month for a year until the jaundice disappeared. After that, I had to have monthly checkups. The doctor would examine me, tell my mom everything was okay, and say, "See you next month." My mom had so much gratitude for Dr. Visco, she went to say goodbye to him before we left for America. At that time, he advised, "When you're in America, take Angelina to the doctor regularly."

The medical examination in Napoli usually took about fifteen minutes, but when it was my turn, I was kept for over an hour, and so was Claudio. The doctor found our blood work abnormal and didn't want to clear us. He called my mother in to tell her, and she pleaded for clearance. "Please, doctor, my children are fine, please clear them so we can go to America." Who knows if it was pure luck, or sympathy for my mom, but the only thing the doctor said was, "If anything should happen to either of your children, you're young enough to take care of them," and he cleared us. Thinking about it now, since both my brother and I were eventually diagnosed with muscular dystrophy after coming to America, the blood test had most likely revealed elevated CPK levels.

Next, we went to the consulate office, which was located in the same building, just a different window. Passports and a date of entry were issued to my parents, and since I was the oldest, my photo went into my mom's passport while the rest of my siblings had only their names entered. We were free to move to the New World!

We finished in Napoli much later than expected. Our time with the doctor had taken so long that we were all starving. My papà and Zio Licandro went to buy panini with mortadella, and we ate it standing on the street.

I don't remember packing. I just wanted to see my mother happy. My mother packed sheets, quilts, pillows, pillow covers made in Italy, and all the clothes my grandmother sent us from America. In fact, the only clothes we packed were those that my grandmother had sent us. Zia Matalena helped organize the clothes as my mom packed them. She also helped my mom sew the burlap packages with thick white thread. Clothes that didn't fit us she gave away to a paisana who was in need.

My mom has told us that we said goodbye to all of our relatives and neighbors. Zia Matalena, who remained in Italy, told my parents, "Good luck. It will be better in America. There is nothing to do in this town."

Zia Rosa, our closest neighbor, who lived down the road from us, was nicknamed Rosa De Teretélla. She came from a wealthy family, my mom from a poor family. They greeted each other as all villagers do, but it stopped there. My mamma wasn't really close to her until she built a house near my grandmother's and they became neighbors. As time went by, they bonded in a special way, even though my grandparents had an argument with Rosa, and *they* all greeted each other in a stubborn way. My mom, having grown up in the convent, didn't get in the middle of such things. She was able to stay in the present. Consequently, my mom and Rosa became the best of friends.

Zia Rosa always wore her hair in a low braid she folded up and fastened on the back of her head with a big barrette. Although most of the villagers wore the town costume, because Zia Rosa's husband went to Venezuela to work and sent her money, she wore regular clothes, like a skirt that went down to the middle of her knees, a knit sweater, and shoes. From the time I remember her, Zia Rosa always had a smile on her face, except if something was sad.

Then you would see the sorrow. She was very, very funny. Her expressions, the way she said things, her loud, giggly laugh. I'm so grateful she was in my mother's life. It gave her some sort of laughter. When my mother had my sister Maria, she asked Zia Rosa to be her godmother, and she said yes. My mamma had the honor of having Zia Rosa as a *comare* for her daughter, and then they were more than just friends. She was my sister's godmother. They greeted each other, "*Buongiorno, cumò* (dialect for *comare*/godmother)," as a sign of respect. So the bond grew even stronger. A godmother in Italy is a sacred thing and a highly respected person by the goddaughter and her family. Zia Rosa knew our situation, and when she found out we were leaving, she said, "Thank God you are being sponsored."

Soon it was time to say goodbye to our relatives in my dad's hometown, Vairano Patenora. As we were walking on the street of Vairano Patenora going to Zia Angelélla Funaro's (my grandmother's sister's) house, we passed by a store that sold dolls. My sister Rita was only five years old, and when she saw the doll, she wanted it. My mom couldn't afford it and said, "Be quiet and walk." Well, Rita started to cry so hard that, when we reached Zia Angelélla Funaro's home, her eyes were still filled with tears, and more tears were rolling down her face. Zia Angelélla was taken aback and said, "Oh, my God!" "Look how this child is crying because she doesn't want to leave us!" Now, when we look back, we think how funny that was.

Every time we visited our relatives, I kissed everyone and said, *"Buonasera."* But now I could say, *"Buonasera.* We're going to America!" My Zia would ask, "Who are you going to find there?" Delighted, I would answer, *"Nonna!"*

Returning to Italy never crossed our minds, except for papà. When saying goodbye to people, he would say, "Don't worry, I'll be back soon." Mama's desperation made her say, "I don't want to return to Italy, not even dead," but deep inside, we all knew she didn't mean it.

Antonio Paolone owned a *pullmanino*, a station wagon, without any specific signs, and he acted as the village taxi. Papà said, "Ciao, ciao," to the house when we were leaving Gallo, as my mom grabbed us and walked straight to Antonio's car. I was the oldest and followed mama's footsteps.

My mom was wearing a blue skirt below her knees and a white knit short-sleeved blouse, black shoes, and, believe it or not, pantyhose. There was one store that sold them. My papà was wearing gray pants, a white shirt, and black shoes. My sisters and I were dressed like triplets in the light-blue dresses that still fit from when my godmother, Caterina Cippolone, had given them to us before she left for America. Claudio, just two years old, was so cute, with his chubby face and legs, wearing shorts above the knee with a T-shirt and vest from my grandmother. He was adorable. His hair was light blond with a big curl the size of an adult finger right in the middle of his head.

We rode away in Antonio Paolone's big station wagon, glancing for the last time at the fields of Gallo Matese, on our way to Napoli.

On the plane, Maria, sitting on my father's lap by the window, slammed her hands on the glass wanting to feel the air outside. Pacifier in his mouth, Claudio slept through the entire flight in my mother's arms.

"Are you tired, Mammà?"

"Yes, I'm tired, but what can I do? Soon we'll be in America."

"Mammà, are we arriving?"

"In a little while."

Putting my hand around my mamma's shoulders and holding Claudio's head, I fell asleep, and Mamma removed my hands. She says that I thought that by putting my hand on Claudio's head, I was helping. But even though I was making it worse, she let me do it to keep me quiet, because if she didn't, I'd keep asking, "Mammà, why don't you want me to help you?" From the age of four, all I wanted to do was help. If we were getting ready to go into the village or to a doctor's appointment, I would insist, "Mammà, let me help you get my sisters ready!"

She would answer, "All right, get me socks."

But not only did I help out, I gave suggestions: "Mammà, this looks better!"

"Okay."

My mother says that, as a child, I had the mentality of an old lady.

We left Gallo Matese at four-thirty a.m. and arrived at the airport in Naples at six a.m. Alitalia flight #610 took off from Naples at eight thirty, stopping in Rome and then Milano to pick up other passengers. This made the flight ten hours instead of eight.

My mother worried that it was a long flight with four children. We fell asleep on and off and didn't like the food, so all we ate were unsalted crackers. Nobody ate anything else except my dad. He ate everything, saying, "Let's start the American way!"

Chapter 21

LITTLE ITALY, THE BRONX, OUR LADY OF MT. CARMEL CHURCH

When I was ten and staying at Nonna's house in the Bronx at 652 East 187th Street with my family while we looked for our first apartment in the United States, I could see Our Lady of Mt. Carmel diagonally across the street from the living room window. Mammuccèlla, my sweet little mother, which is the name I started calling Mòma in New York, was pleased to live so near the church. The first thing she did was get me involved in Il Circolo Cattolico Italiano, the Italian Catholic Club, run by the *Ancelle della Divina Misericordia*,[65] who were all from Italy. This meant that I was also part of the choir. Every Friday, we met in a small

65.   Sisters of the Divine Mercy.

building behind the church where the Ancelle lived. The church quickly became my hangout, and I sang with the choir at the eight and eleven a.m. Italian masses. The nine and ten a.m. masses were in English. My favorite was the eleven a.m., because instead of singing downstairs with the rest of the congregation, we sang from the balcony, where Grace played the organ. I loved singing way up in the choir loft, as the acoustics of the church carried our voices, with the loud organ music, to all the parishioners.

Surrounded by this halo of familiar culture and tradition, I felt at home, and although I was awed by the grandeur of the church, with its stained-glass windows and Roman marble columns dividing the pews into four sections, I took comfort in the familiar faces of saints I'd loved since infancy. On the right side of the altar was la Madonnina, Immaculate Conception, and on the left, St. Anthony of Padua. And, like our church in Italy, on each wall were paintings of the twelve Stations of the Cross.

Soon, my favorite spot to pray was in the front of the church, on the left side in an alcove located outside the priest's room, where there was a large painting of beautiful women weeping with their arms outstretched, pleading to be saved from the burning flames of purgatory. Mammuccèlla told me to pray for them, because my prayers would reduce their days in purgatory and help them get to heaven sooner. Any chance I had, I'd pray in front of the painting over and over *L'Eterno Riposo*, eternal rest, so they wouldn't have to suffer much longer.

Another sacred place I visited all the time with my parents those first summers in New York also reminded me of Italy. This was la Madonnina di Lourdes located in the grotto outside of St. Lucy's Church on Pelham Parkway. The statue was elevated in an old stone sanctuary, with holy water seeping through its rocks and flowing into a shallow pond. I have loved the story of Bernadette and Our Lady of Lourdes from the time I was very young and my mammuccèlla gave me a prayer card with a picture of the small French girl kneeling before an apparition of la Madonnina.

Every night for years, I held the card when I said my bedtime prayers, and secretly wanted to be like Bernadette. My mother's strategy worked to bring me more deeply into the Catholic faith, which has been such an important part of her life story.

Chapter 22

ITALIA MIA

I've always paid attention to what people are wearing, especially women, and thought for a long time that this was because of the years of poverty in Gallo combined with moving to the United States, where everyone dressed so differently. When I landed in Little Italy at ten years of age, in many ways, it felt like home because nearly everyone was southern Italian. A mixture of newcomers from different areas merged with those whose families had been in the United States for years, or even one or two generations. This created economic and dialect differences, but for the most part, we all shared the same cultural and religious beliefs, which made life a bit easier when we didn't speak a word of English. In school, I became familiar with different Italian dialects and adapted. However, there was a big difference in how I dressed, which didn't feel good, but without money, my appearance seemed hopeless.

On the positive side, my love of watching people and noticing how they dressed served me well in my first job, after school and on Saturdays, at Terrigno's, a local discount store, where I learned a lot by observing the working people. Every day was like a fashion show. Coming from such a remote village, I had never seen so many different fashions. There was always a stream of customers shopping, getting their photos developed, or even playing the Lotto.

At fourteen, I was the youngest person working in the store, but I loved it. Even though I was shy, I followed all instructions closely and never had to be asked to do anything twice. Terrigno's felt like family and as if I was working in my own home.

Cora and Nick Terrigno owned the store. They had two daughters, Evelyn and Jo-Ann, who were beautiful, spoke perfect English, and were very fashionable. I looked up to them. Each day, one, the other, or both would come to the store after their college classes and work the cash register. They also worked in the store on Saturdays, and so did Nick, who was with a construction company during the week. Cora was the only one who worked full-time in the store, and she was a terrific boss. The family was very generous, and on Saturdays, which were always extra busy, they made delicious hero sandwiches for the employees' lunch. And each Saturday, Nick drove me home and made sure that I left with a bag of candies for my family.

Even more exciting for me were the packages of clothing from the girls whenever they updated their wardrobes. On those occasions, Nick carried the large bag of clothing on his back like Santa Claus, up the long flight of stairs to

our apartment. The minute he left, my sisters and I rushed into the living room and opened the bag, looking at all the clothes. We tried them on and picked out what fit each of us the best, so that we all had new outfits. It was thrilling! The Terrignos also gave me gifts for my birthday and Christmas. I loved their sense of style and good taste, and everything they gave me was special. I feel as if I grew up in that store.

A few times, Cora invited my entire family to their beautiful house near Palmer Road in Yonkers. She cooked in their open kitchen with her elderly mother, and I was amazed by how much more space they had than we did in our apartment. One time, I saw a woman in a blue dress with a white apron and a feather duster in her hand, cleaning. After thinking about it for a while, I realized she was a cleaning lady. I had never seen one. I remember sitting with the Terrignos on the couch in their living room, surrounded by stylish furniture and feeling so honored and comfortable.

I still think of Jo-Ann Terrigno, who was thin, beautiful, and always dancing. From the cash register, her little radio always played hit songs from the '70s, and whenever she had the chance, she and her boyfriend, Anthony, practiced the Hustle in the back room.

Evelyn was the older sister and more on the serious side. She had an exquisite wedding where, for the first time in my life, I heard someone playing a harp.

It amuses me now to think about the pecking order that existed in Italian communities, but in my youth, it caused me pain both in Italy and in the United States. In Little Italy, even though we all came from southern Italy, *Il Mezzogiorno*, the Land of Midday Sun, and the poorest region in the European Union where industry remains firmly rooted in agriculture, there were hierarchies.

Historically, southern Italians have been considered poor peasants and inferior or low-class compared to the northern Italians from the industrial heartland who had no financial need to emigrate from Italy to other countries. This inequality between north and south created friction even among Italians who came to the United States. I was very aware of being excluded, and I noticed the way class friction existed sometimes within the southern Italian community itself. But, of course, having muscular dystrophy heightens my sensitivity to exclusion.

In retrospect, I learned more about Italy living in New York. Looking back at these stories, I realize that they are a way for me to return to Italy any time I want.

ITALIA MIA

Across the ocean
my dreams have been shattered.
I would like
to hug you right now
with your culture
that illuminated the world.

Rich was my garden of sour plums
and cherries
pollinated by wind and honeybees.
At sunset,
tired men return from the grazing fields.
Unforgettably curved backs,
deeply wrinkled faces
glow with pride.

A candle in the center of the table,
vivid eyes on the frattaccio,
and after dinner, around the fireplace
listening to elders' stories,
we learn about life.
Into the night, little girls follow the tradition
of chasing fireflies and counting stars.

Venus, the morning star
appears at dawn,
cuckoo, cuckoo, the rooster of Zia Rosa
wakes me to sparrow chirps.

The uninterrupted wings of butterflies
with no clear path
never tire, resting on one
or another flower
savoring each unique taste.

Before breakfast,
taking eggs from the chicken coop,
giving them to Mamma
to transform into frittatas for all of us
along with homemade bread.

Overwhelmed by events of life,
though once so fully satisfied,
I could never deny my roots,
my desire for you
has no end,
Italia mia.[66]

66.   Poem *Italia Mia* by Angela D'Arezzo.

Acknowledgments

We have many people to acknowledge for their help with *The Salty Mountain*. First, we want to thank each other. Angela's gratitude to me for working with her and making this book possible, and mine, to her, for her creative spirit, passion, and tenacity and the trust she showed me in her desire to share, as well as her willingness to explore further the powerful themes and relationships that have inspired and shaped her life, reflect the intrinsic camaraderie of this project.

While the book itself is an affirmation of the love and devotion Angela feels for her parents, it is important to her that she convey, in these acknowledgments, her gratitude to Rosa and Antonio D'Arezzo. Their support, strength, encouragement, and being there for her always, as well as the motivation of her siblings, made everything possible.

Thank you to Kala (Krista) Smith for her Visible Theater True Story Project, where Angela's interest in storytelling and writing began, and, for furthering Angela's insights, to Stacey Engels, Visible Theater's creative writing workshop teacher.

Many family members and friends provided memories and detailed information that helped us bring these stories to life, especially about Gallo Matese. We are especially indebted to Raffaele Gianfrancesco for his dedication in helping with the stories of Vairano Patenora.

The assistance of my friends and family was also profound. Margot Lewis, Deborah Kelly, and Bob Appel cannot be thanked enough for their dedication and time spent reading countless drafts, for helping with research and all of the practical details in bringing *The Salty Mountain* to publication.

Barbara Maria, with contributions from Cecilia Fontanesi and Ondine Appel, created a wonderful video for Overtime Dance Foundation, Inc. This archival and promotional material was a vital part of our *Salty Mountain* online fundraising campaign. Successfully initiated and managed by Lianna King, the campaign enabled us to achieve our goal.

Everyone connected with this book has deep appreciation for the artwork of Naima Rauam, who is known for her watercolors of the South Street Seaport historic district in New York City. Her Gallo Matese cover painting and illustrations provide an authentic and eloquent visual frame for the historical narrative, *The Salty Mountain*.

Overtime Dance Foundation, Inc. is a non-profit tax-exempt organization devoted to supporting the creative work of artists, individuals and groups who make fearless connections through embodied expression that help us to experience and understand the world and ourselves.

www.overtimedancefoundation.org

ANGELA D'AREZZO came to the United States with her family from Gallo Matese, a village in the Campania Region of Italy, when she was ten years old. Her avid interest in the arts led her to perform in dance and theater with NTWH and Visible Theater True Story Project in New York City and Belfast, Maine. She was a spokesperson for the Muscular Dystrophy Association, a part-time model, and appeared on the cover of *Quest*, a Muscular Dystrophy Society publication. She was also featured in an article in *NYU Physician*, "Empowering Women with Disabilities," speaking about her passion for dance and her love of the tarantella as a child in Italy.

CATHY APPEL is a dancer, choreographer, clinician, writer and editor, with extensive experience in project, curriculum and program development. She has performed in many venues, such as New York City Center, The Esplanade in Boston and the Academy of Music in Philadelphia. Her writing has been published in literary and research journals, anthologies and textbooks, and she has presented her clinical and academic work nationally and internationally. She is the President/Artistic Director of Overtime Dance Foundation, Inc.

NAIMA RAUAM is an artist who has followed her passion for place throughout a successful career. She came to New York City at 18 to study at the Art Students League where, as the result of a class assignment, she fell in love with the Fulton Fish Market. Naima also lived and painted in Maine for a period. Naima is most recognized for her watercolors of the South Street Seaport historic district and the Fulton Fish Market, which she has documented with her artwork since the mid 1960s. She also works in oil, charcoal, pastel and graphite.

www.artpm.com